ELVIS PRESLEY MEMPHIS

Mark P. Bernardo

MusicPlace Series

ROARING FORTIES
PRESS

Roaring Forties Press
1053 Santa Fe Avenue
Berkeley, California, 94706

Library of Congress Cataloging-in-Publication Data
Library of Congress Cataloging-in-Publication Data

Bernardo, Mark P., 1969-
  Elvis Presley : Memphis / Mark P. Bernardo.
      p. cm. -- (MusicPlace series)
  Includes bibliographical references.
  ISBN 978-0-9846239-0-7 (pbk. : alk. paper) -- ISBN 978-1-938901-00-3 (epub)
-- ISBN 978-1-938901-01-0 (kindle) -- ISBN 978-1-938901-02-7 (pdf) 1. Pres-
ley, Elvis, 1935-1977--Homes and haunts--Tennessee--Memphis. I. Title.
  ML420.P96B53 2012
  782.42166092--dc23
  [B]
                            2011037027

contents

acknowledgments

This book could not have been possible without the work of numerous other writers and researchers that preceded it, primarily Peter Guralnick's definitive two-volume biography of Elvis, *Last Train to Memphis* and *Careless Love*. Other Elvis biographers and confidants whose work was helpful include Alanna Nash, Billy Smith, Marty Lacker, Lamar Fike, Priscilla Presley, Peter Harry Brown, Pat H. Broeske, and Robert Gordon. *Frommer's Nashville and Memphis* was both a great source of Memphis information and an invaluable tool in planning my research trips to the city. Many newspaper and magazine articles, both historic and recent, also provided useful material.

Scotty Moore's website (www.scottymoore.com) was an incredible resource for tracking down information on many of the sites listed in the book, particularly the ones that have since disappeared. Other notable Web sources included the Elvis Information Network (www.elvisinfonet.com) and the Australian Elvis fan site (www.elvispresley.com.au), a treasure trove of meticulously researched Elvis history. Valuable information on the Loew's State Theatre and other movie theaters came from www.cinematreasures.com.

Special recognition is due to Hal Lansky of Lansky Brothers Clothiers, who kindly took time out of a busy day at the Lansky Brothers store to show me around and answer questions about his family and Elvis Presley; Kelly Earnest, public relations director at the Peabody Hotel, who made sure our stay in Memphis was both comfortable and informative; Jason Sensat, the current Peabody Duckmaster, who provided historical tidbits and insights into the hotel; Jayne White, publicity director at Sun Studio; Bill Patton of Backbeat Tours (and author of *A Guide to Historic Downtown Memphis*), a font of knowledge about Memphis history who filled in information gaps about numerous sites in this book and contributed a few more that weren't originally on my list; Jackie Reed, communications manager for the Memphis Convention and Visitors Bureau; "Memphis" Jones, the singing raconteur who led our tour around the city; my publishers, Deirdre Greene and Nigel Quinney at Roaring Forties Press, for their enthusiastic support of this project and dedication to making it the best it could be; and my wife, partner, research assistant, and fellow Elvis fan, Holly, for her unfailing encouragement.

city of memphis

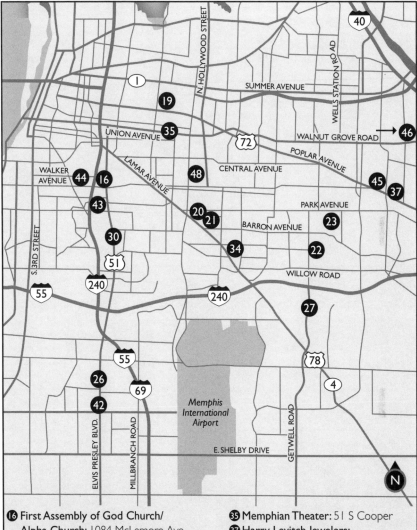

🔟 **First Assembly of God Church/
Alpha Church:** 1084 McLemore Ave.

🔟 **Overton Park Shell/Levitt Shell:**
1930 Poplar Ave., in Overton Park

🔟 **Lamar Airways Shopping Center**

🔟 **Presleys' sixth home:** 2414 Lamar Ave.*

🔟 **Presleys' seventh home:** 1414 Getwell Rd.*

🔟 **Presleys' eighth home:** 1034 Audubon Dr.

🔟 **Graceland:** 3764 Elvis Presley Blvd.

🔟 **Kennedy Veterans Hospital:** 3000 Getwell Rd.

🔟 **Forest Hill Cemetery:** 1661 Elvis Presley Blvd.

🔟 **Rainbow Rollerdrome:** 2895 Lamar Ave.*

🔟 **Memphian Theater:** 51 S Cooper

🔟 **Harry Levitch Jewelers:**
5100 Poplar Ave.

🔟 **Gridiron:** 4101 Elvis Presley Blvd.

🔟 **Coletta's:** 1063 S Parkway E

🔟 **Stax Records/Stax Museum of
American Soul Music:**
926 East McLemore Ave.

🔟 **Lowell Hays & Sons:** 4872 Poplar Ave.*

🔟 **Master Kang Rhee Institute:**
706 Germantown Pkwy.

🔟 **Libertyland:** 940 Early Maxwell Blvd.*

*Indicates that this is the former location of the site, which has now closed or moved.

downtown memphis, west side

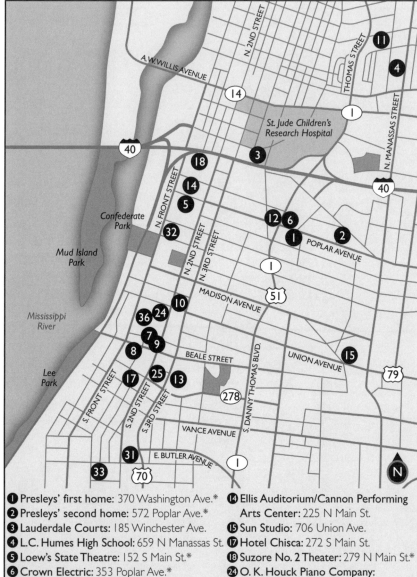

1. **Presleys' first home:** 370 Washington Ave.*
2. **Presleys' second home:** 572 Poplar Ave.*
3. **Lauderdale Courts:** 185 Winchester Ave.
4. **L.C. Humes High School:** 659 N Manassas St.*
5. **Loew's State Theatre:** 152 S Main St.*
6. **Crown Electric:** 353 Poplar Ave.*
7. **Blues City Café:** 138 Beale St.
8. **Orpheum Theatre:** 203 S Main St.
9. **Lansky Brothers Clothiers:** 126 Beale St.*
10. **Peabody Hotel:** 149 Union Ave.
11. **Presleys' fourth home:** 698 Saffarans St.*
12. **Poplar Tunes:** 308 Poplar Ave.*
13. **Memphis Rock & Soul Museum:** 191 Beale St.
14. **Ellis Auditorium/Cannon Performing Arts Center:** 225 N Main St.
15. **Sun Studio:** 706 Union Ave.
17. **Hotel Chisca:** 272 S Main St.
18. **Suzore No. 2 Theater:** 279 N Main St*
24. **O. K. Houck Piano Company:** 121 Union Ave.*
25. **Gibson:** 145 Lt. George W. Lee Ave.
31. **Union Station**
32. **Claridge Hotel:** 109 N Main St.
33. **Arcade:** 540 S Main St.
36. **Jolly Royal Furniture Store:** 128 S Main St.

*Indicates that this is the former location of the site, which has now closed or moved.

downtown memphis, east side

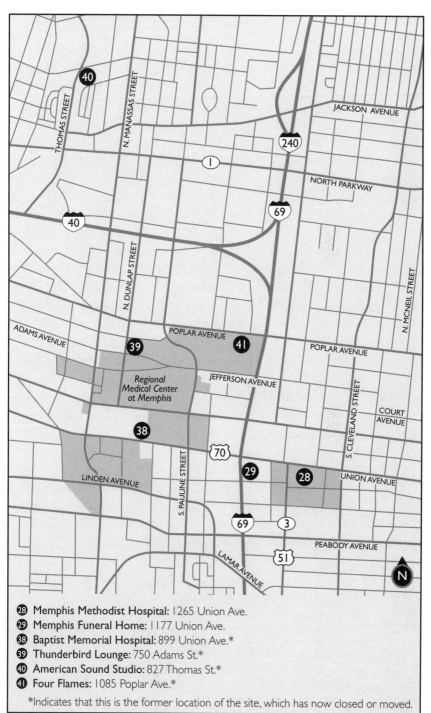

28 Memphis Methodist Hospital: 1265 Union Ave.
29 Memphis Funeral Home: 1177 Union Ave.
38 Baptist Memorial Hospital: 899 Union St.*
39 Thunderbird Lounge: 750 Adams St.*
40 American Sound Studio: 827 Thomas St.*
41 Four Flames: 1085 Poplar Ave.*

*Indicates that this is the former location of the site, which has now closed or moved.

ELVIS PRESLEY MEMPHIS

Main Street, Memphis, 1950s.

chapter 1

building the bluff city

"What did I miss about Memphis? Everything."
— Elvis Presley, 1960, after his discharge from the
U.S. Army

You can tell a lot about a city just by visiting its airport. Las Vegas's McCarran International Airport is full of slot machines and has huge murals of nightclub acts. Miami International Airport greets its visitors with faux palm trees and sunny pastels. When you disembark at Memphis International Airport, the symbols of the city's identity await you near the baggage claim carousels, in a kiosk featuring three vintage musical instruments mounted in front of large photos of their owners: blues legend B. B. King, soul icon Isaac Hayes, and Elvis Presley, both the King of Rock 'n' Roll and, arguably, the originator of it.

Rock 'n' roll means something much different today than it did when Elvis was a teen. The modern term conjures images of raucous arenas, enormous drum sets, and massive amplifiers. Rock stars today are often regarded as pampered, overindulged celebrities, surrounded by bodyguards, staying in opulent hotel rooms with easy access to drugs, booze, and wall-to-wall groupies. Several of these stereotypes started with Elvis during his self-destructive later years.

How ironic, then, that rock 'n' roll began in a modest, two-story brick recording studio, in a mid-South city that made its musical reputation on Delta blues and hillbilly music. And that the young man who became its symbol was a poor, shy kid from rural Mississippi whose primary musical love was gospel and whose first albums didn't even have a drummer.

Memphis, Tennessee, was instrumental in bringing blues, gospel, soul, rockabilly, and, yes, rock 'n' roll, to mainstream popularity in America. All these musical genres are woven into the city's historical tapestry and remain essential elements of its identity today, but only rock 'n' roll can trace its origins to the city itself. Elvis Presley and his legendary career are the common thread that runs through all these musical styles. The day that a twenty-year-old truck driver for Crown Electric came in to Sam Phillips's Sun Records recording studio to (legend has it) make a record for his beloved mama was the beginning of a musical movement that would dominate popular music, and society at large, for generations, and would take Elvis Presley on a meteoric journey from local hero to worldwide phenomenon. And yet, while rock 'n' roll itself outgrew the city of its birth, Elvis never fully uprooted himself from his adopted hometown. For Elvis Presley, the first rock star, whether he was making movies in Hollywood or playing sold-out shows in Vegas, Memphis was home; from his youngest days, the music of his hometown was his inspiration.

Yet, to focus only on the music while ignoring the events that inspired it would be to paint an incomplete picture of Memphis's musical heritage. Nothing exists in a vacuum, and no musical tradition emerges out of thin air. To understand the music of Memphis, and the profound role that it played in both the history of the city and the shaping of its most famous musical icon, one must understand the turbulence and struggles from which that music arose.

overton's dream

The wooded bluffs overlooking the Mississippi River had long been the home of several Native American tribes, primarily the Chickasaw, even before it was said to be the site of Spanish explorer Hernando de Soto's "discovery" of the Mississippi in 1541. The land on which Memphis stands once contained a French fort, Fort Assumption, and a Spanish fort, San Fernando de los Barrancas. The Tennessee territory, of which Memphis was the westernmost sector, was part of North Carolina in 1783, when that state's government, despite the Chickasaws' claims to it, opened the area to settlement. (Tennessee became a state and was admitted into the Union in 1796.) In a prelude to the racial struggles that would plague Memphis in the nineteenth and twentieth centuries, European settlers and Native Americans clashed over ownership of the land for several decades.

A European named John Rice bought 5,000 acres of the western Tennessee territory—essentially the site of modern-day downtown Memphis—from the North Carolina state government in 1783. Rice was later killed in an attack by Native Americans, and his brother inherited the land, eventually selling it to a small group of land speculators led by a Nashville lawyer named John Overton.

Overton, regarded as the most important of the city's founders and something of a patron saint of Memphis—Overton Park is named after him—was born in Virginia in 1766 and began his law career in present-day Kentucky in 1787. He moved to Nashville in 1789 and was admitted to the Tennessee bar a year later. His first roommate was another young lawyer who would go on to greater things: Andrew Jackson. The two became lifelong friends and, eventually, partners in land speculation. In 1789, Overton represented Sumner County at North Carolina's convention to ratify the U.S. Constitution. Jackson became Tennessee's first congressman in 1796 and went on to become a military hero in the early 1800s, leading U.S. forces in the wars against the Indians and defeating the British in the War of 1812 at the Battle of New Orleans.

Overton not only promoted Jackson's political career—Jackson became the seventh U.S. president in 1828—but succeeded him on the Tennessee Superior Court (the forerunner of today's Tennessee Supreme Court) in 1804. Overton partnered with Jackson and another military hero, General James Winchester, to purchase a tract of land known as the Chickasaw Bluffs, near the confluence of the Mississippi and Wolf Rivers, on which the city of Memphis would be founded on May 22, 1819. Winchester, a lover of antiquities, suggested naming it after the Egyptian city on the Nile. (In 1991, developers took the Egyptian motif to a new level when they erected the Pyramid Arena in the downtown area on the banks of the Mississippi. Once Memphis's premier sports venue, the arena is little used today, although it dominates the Memphis skyline.)

The Americans rightly saw that the location of the land—high above the floodplain of the Mississippi—would make it an ideal point for trade and transportation as well as a natural fort against attackers and barrier against flooding. In 1845, the city established a naval yard; in 1857, the Memphis and Charleston Railroad was completed, linking Memphis with Charleston, South Carolina, a port city on the Atlantic Ocean. Memphis soon became one of the most important ports in the country for cotton grown in the Mississippi Delta, the South's primary cash crop.

war and plague

The booming cotton trade of the nineteenth century helped call the nation's attention to the issue of slavery. Much of Memphis's economy, like that of the rest of the antebellum South, revolved around cotton, an industry largely dependent on slave labor, and much of

Overton's wealth came from the slave trade. With the specter of civil war looming in the mid-1800s, it was inevitable that even one of the South's largest, most prosperous cities would be torn apart by the nationwide debate over the issue.

Tennessee seceded from the Union in 1861, and the city of Memphis mustered up enough citizen-soldiers—between one-third and one-fourth of the population—for seventy-two companies in the new Confederate army. However, Memphis's role as a Confederate stronghold was short-lived. In 1862, in the Battle of Memphis, the Union fleet defeated the Confederate navy, and Union troops occupied the city, swiftly establishing it as a headquarters, supply depot, and detention facility for Confederate prisoners of war. General Grant, who led the Union army, set up operations there in 1863, using the city as a support base for the attack on Vicksburg. Thus, with martial law declared, Memphis was a Union outpost for most of the Civil War, which ended in 1865. It even established public schools for freed black slaves. Many blacks settled in the southern part of Memphis after the war, making it one of the first cities in America to have a true African American community, and hence giving Memphis a head start among Southern cities in the area of race relations.

War was not the only problem facing Memphis in the nineteenth century. There were no fewer than six outbreaks of yellow fever, the first of which hit the city soon after its founding, in 1828, infecting 650 and killing 150. As Memphis's population grew, the death counts from subsequent outbreaks rose. The second epidemic, in 1855, was more devastating, with 220 fatalities out of 1,250 infected. The third came on the heels of the race riots that followed the end of the war, in 1867. This one was even more overwhelming, killing 550 people. But it was only a prelude to the ravages of the next two epidemics, which hit in 1873 (5,000 cases, 2,000 deaths) and in 1878 (more than 5,000 deaths). No one knew how to cure or prevent the disease, or even that it was spread by infected mosquitoes, and so the populace could only try to flee or tough it out.

These dark days of plague are commemorated at Martyr's Park, on Channel 3 Drive, off Riverside Drive, just north of the I-55 bridge on the Mississippi riverfront. The park is dedicated to the brave doctors, nurses, priests, ministers, and other civilian volunteers who stayed in the ravaged city during the yellow fever outbreaks to care for the victims and bury the dead.

The epidemics took their toll on the city's economy: Memphis declared bankruptcy and lost its city charter in 1879. That same year, yet another yellow fever outbreak occurred (this one killing 200 people), finally spurring the Tennessee state government, which now ran the city as a taxing district, to take some kind of action. Under the guidance of Dr. P. T. Porter, who had theorized that the city's poor sanitation systems were at fault, the state established public health programs and initiatives (including cleaning up open sewers and building artesian wells for water) that destroyed the plague-carrying mosquitoes' breeding grounds and shielded the city from the disease.

The yellow fever outbreaks helped to determine Memphis's racial identity and, by extension, its music. The black population in Memphis quadrupled between 1860 and 1870, and for reasons never fully understood, of the thousands of people who perished in the 1878 epidemic, fewer than 20 percent were black.

the boss and the blues

Things began looking up in Memphis when the city emerged from bankruptcy and regained its charter in 1893. Following the end of the Civil War, and subsequent passage of the Reconstruction Act of 1867, the Fifteenth Amendment in 1870, and the Civil Rights Act of 1875, blacks had the right to vote and to have equal access to education, homes, and services. However, an undercurrent of racism remained in the still-healing United States, particularly in the defeated Southern states; the landmark *Plessy vs. Ferguson* Supreme Court decision of 1896, which upheld the legitimacy of black-white segregation (as long as the facilities were "separate but equal"), ushered in the so-called Jim Crow laws, which mandated that blacks and whites eat at separate counters, drink from separate fountains, attend separate schools, and generally avoid racially mixed activities. This institutionalized segregation persisted throughout the first half of the twentieth century.

Although former slaves and their descendants maintained the right to vote during the Jim Crow era, they could not easily exercise that right. In the early post-Reconstruction period, federal troops were often called in to protect black voters from intimidation. In 1865, the white supremacist Ku Klux Klan was formed; members of this group favored the use of violence, terror, and even murder to prevent blacks from exercising their rights.

The Jim Crow laws were enforced mostly in the South. In Memphis, the racial divide expressed itself in its music. Whites listened to classical or "hillbilly" country music; blacks listened to genres that had emerged from the slave days: blues and gospel. Eventually, radio stations and record companies tailored their material for either a white or a black audience, rarely crossing over. Until Elvis came along, few if any artists tried to break down those barriers.

Memphis's black citizens gained a powerful friend with the emergence of the influential political figure Edward H. "Boss" Crump, who, for good or ill, made the city synonymous with machine politics. Crump was a successful businessman who began establishing a network of political connections in the late nineteenth century, a network that he used to progress from one political office to another: from state Democratic convention delegate in 1902 and 1904, to a seat on the Board of Public Works in 1905, to commissioner of fire and police in 1907, all the way to mayor of Memphis in 1910.

Crump, who—unlike many other Southern Democrats at the time—supported the rights of blacks to vote, built a powerful coalition by appealing to the two other groups that sided with him on the issue: blacks and Republicans. Both were in the minority in Tennessee at the time, but together they made up a sizeable voting bloc. The strategy proved successful and made Crump's Democratic machine a political juggernaut. Crump served three two-year terms as mayor from 1910 to

1915 and maintained a behind-the-scenes influence until 1940, as the machine he constructed continued to play a decisive role in running the city. Crump hand-picked several of the mayors who followed him, became the U.S. representative from Shelby County, and served on the Democratic National Committee. Crump's legacy includes the city's Crump Stadium and Crump Boulevard, its well-regarded fire department, its annual automobile safety inspections, and—somewhat ironically in a city known for music—its strict noise ordinances.

Boss Crump's first election as Memphis mayor is inextricably tied to a seminal event in the city's musical history. As Crump was campaigning in 1909, another important twentieth-century figure—one who would have a direct influence on the music that inspired Elvis Presley—was making his presence known in the smoky bars and clubs of black-dominated Beale Street. William Christopher ("W. C.") Handy is regarded as the father of the blues, and was the most important figure in popularizing the genre—which had evolved from the work songs and "field hollers" of black slaves working on Southern plantations in the nineteenth century—throughout the United States.

Handy wrote "Mr. Crump," the campaign song for Crump's first run for mayor, a song widely credited with playing a role in Crump's election. In 1912, Handy rewrote the popular song and changed its name to "Memphis Blues." He sold the rights to a music publisher in 1912 for $100, making this song the first published commercial blues song. "Memphis Blues" became a nationwide hit, earning the publisher (but not Handy) a lot of money. The experience inspired Handy to get into the music publishing business himself, and he published his subsequent blues hits—"St. Louis Blues" and "Yellow Dog Blues," both in 1914, and "Beale Street Blues," in 1916—under his own label, Handy Music Company. After several years of success in Memphis, Handy moved to New York in 1918; from then until 1940 (when he went blind), he used his resources and fame to promote blues music and publish collections of music by African American artists. He died of pneumonia in 1958, the same year Elvis Presley enlisted in the army.

W. C. Handy, like Overton, Crump, and Elvis, is considered one of Memphis's icons, and visitors to the city can find several tributes to him. W. C. Handy Performing Arts Park, at 200 Beale Street at Third Avenue, across from the FedEx Forum, hosts live music performances at its Pepsi Pavilion, an open-air amphitheater with a capacity of 800. Patrons can also have a drink at the outdoor Handy Bar. A bronze statue of the legendary bluesman with his signature instrument, a cornet, stands at one end of the park. The two-room clapboard shotgun shack where Handy lived when he wrote "Memphis Blues" and "Beale Street Blues" still stands at 352 Beale at the corner of Fourth Avenue, and has been preserved as the W. C. Handy House and Museum. Visitors can tour the house and see the tiny desk where Handy wrote his songs, as well as other memorabilia.

The Blues Foundation, a nonprofit group dedicated to preserving and honoring blues history, headquartered at 49 Union Avenue in Memphis, acknowledged the influence of the blues on rock 'n' roll in 1984 when it awarded its W. C. Handy Award (now known as the Blues Music Award) posthumously to Elvis for "keeping the blues alive . . . in rock and roll."

In the wake of the blues came gospel, which also has roots in the days of slavery. Although it is similar to blues in its rhythms and vocals, gospel shows the influence of European church music; unlike blues, whose lyrics tend to focus on secular themes of heartbreak, poverty, and emotional distress, gospel's themes are uplifting and spiritual, with lyrics that appeal directly to God, Jesus, or the Holy Spirit. Gospel is at home in houses of worship, whereas blues inhabits bars and clubs. Churches and bars are both plentiful in Memphis, so both musical genres thrived.

By the 1920s, the advent of radio was exposing gospel to a wider audience. Reverend Herbert Brewster of Memphis's East Trigg Baptist Church, who wrote popular gospel songs in the 1930s for the likes of Mahalia Jackson and the Ward Singers, and Memphis native Lucie Campbell, who wrote more than a hundred songs and contributed to one of the first gospel songbooks published, are among the city's gospel music figures. The influence of gospel on Elvis Presley was perhaps more profound than that of any other style of music thanks to the Blackwood Brothers, a Memphis gospel quartet whose music he adored throughout his life.

In the 1950s, Elvis and other artists at the legendary Sun Studio played rockabilly and rock 'n' roll, the first musical genres to blend elements of "white" and "black" music. Other musical innovations would follow from Memphis, including soul music, which came of age at the Stax recording studio, whose most famous star was Otis Redding. Elvis, a lifelong fan of many black artists in various musical genres, recorded three albums at Stax in 1973.

blacks and rights

The success of W. C. Handy and the rising popularity of blues and gospel music mirrored the growing prominence of African Americans in Memphis society in the early twentieth century, an era defined largely by racial struggles.

Robert Reed Church, Sr., a real estate entrepreneur turned politician and philanthropist, was Memphis's first black millionaire. In 1893, he bought the first municipal bonds issued by the city of Memphis after its emergence from bankruptcy. In 1899, he opened Church's Park and Auditorium, the first urban entertainment and recreational center catering to black youths. In 1906, he founded the Solvent Bank and Trust Company, the first black-owned bank in Memphis in the twentieth century. Other milestones followed Church's death in 1912, such as the city's first African American community library, built in 1934.

Beale Street became the center of black music and black culture in general. People of color flocked to the boulevard not only to play music, following in the footsteps of Handy, but also to establish businesses. A riverfront park at the end of Beale Street commemorates a great moment of race relations in the dark days of segregation, as well as a man who is regarded as one of Memphis's greatest heroes. Tom

Lee Park is named for a black man who saved the lives of thirty-two white sailors in the Mississippi River on May 8, 1925. Lee, a levee worker, was riding in a small motorboat when he witnessed the steamer *M. E. Norman* capsize. Despite not knowing how to swim, and facing the danger of his own boat sinking in the rough waters, Lee pulled every survivor he could from the river and ferried them to safety on the riverbank, making five trips to shore. He even built a fire to keep the survivors warm while he took his boat back out to recover bodies; despite his efforts, twenty-three people died. Lee was honored by the Engineers' Club of Memphis, which raised money to purchase a house for him and his wife. After Lee died in 1952, the park along the river was named in his honor. The city erected an obelisk monument to Lee with the inscription "A Very Worthy Negro." In 2006, the current monument was erected: a statue of Lee rescuing one of the sailors, surrounded by thirty-two lights representing those rescued that night.

Despite events such as the *M. E. Norman* rescue, though, in the century following the Civil War, the racial tension that followed the South's defeat continued to simmer beneath the surface. Segregation remained common in many establishments through the 1950s.

new century, new ideas

By the twentieth century, cotton was no longer king in Memphis, a city that became the launching pad for a handful of revolutionary business ideas that have shaped modern culture.

Many people today who fill their shopping carts at supermarkets are probably unaware of the debt they owe to an iconoclastic Memphian named Clarence Saunders. Before 1916, grocery store customers brought a list to a store clerk and waited for the clerk to gather the items from the store shelves to fill the order. Saunders saw this system as slow and inefficient and conceived the idea of a store where shoppers could serve themselves. He opened the first Piggly Wiggly—to this day, no one is sure where he came up with the name—at 79 Jefferson Avenue at Main Street. The innovative store offered shopping baskets that customers could fill from open shelves. Piggly Wiggly, now a huge franchise, with more than 600 stores in seventeen states throughout the Southeast and Midwest, was the first grocery retailer to price every item in the store, use refrigerated cases to keep produce fresher longer, provide checkout stands, and require employees to wear uniforms.

The original Piggly Wiggly is no more, but Saunders's legacy lives on in the Pink Palace, a grand but unfinished mansion of pink Georgia marble that he began building at 3050 Central Avenue in 1922. The next year, Saunders went bankrupt in a stock market gamble, lost control of the Piggly Wiggly company, and was never able to finish construction. His creditors donated the building to the city, which opened it in 1930 as the Memphis Museum of Natural History and Industrial Arts. In 1967, its nickname became its official name—the Pink Palace Museum—and its many exhibits today include a replica of the first Piggly Wiggly store in Memphis.

In 1952, another Memphis entrepreneur got a visionary business idea from a bad travel experience. Charles Kemmons Wilson, disappointed with the low quality of the roadside motels he had experienced on a family vacation to Washington, D.C., conceived of a chain of standardized motels that would be consistently clean, comfortable, and child-friendly. The first Holiday Inn—named after the Bing Crosby Christmas film—opened for business on August 1, 1952, on Summer Avenue in Memphis. It was so successful that Wilson opened several more shortly thereafter on roads leading into the city. Holiday Inns featured amenities that were far from standard at the time in roadside motor lodges: air-conditioned rooms, in-room telephones, swimming pools, restaurants, and wall-to-wall carpeting. The Holiday Inn became a staple of modern middle-class life in the age of interstate travel. One of Wilson's friends and investors was Sun Records founder Sam Phillips, the man who released Elvis Presley's first singles.

In 1962, Danny Thomas, star of the TV series *Make Room for Daddy* and *The Danny Thomas Show*, joined with a group of Memphis businessmen to establish one of Memphis's largest employers: St. Jude's Children's Research Hospital, which focuses on the research and treatment of childhood diseases and to this day is a leading force in cancer treatment. The name comes from a pledge Thomas made in 1941, when the then-struggling entertainer knelt in front of a statue of St. Jude, the patron saint of hopeless causes. Thomas promised that he would build a shrine to St. Jude if the saint would show him the right direction in life. Thomas's first big break in show business came shortly thereafter. The St. Jude's complex spans a large area of downtown Memphis and includes the gold-domed ALSAC Pavilion, headquarters of the American Lebanese Syrian Associated Charities, the fund-raising organization that Thomas, who is of Arab descent, founded in 1957.

The modern business that has become Memphis's biggest economic engine is FedEx, whose cargo airline, FedEx Express, is based at Memphis International Airport. Founded in Little Rock, Arkansas, in 1971, the company originally known as Federal Express moved to Memphis in 1973. Today it is Memphis's largest private employer, with 32,000 employees. In 2003, the company bought the naming rights to the FedEx Forum, a huge sports arena at 191 Beale Street that is home to the NBA's Memphis Grizzlies and the NCAA's University of Memphis Tigers men's basketball team.

It is Memphis's music, however, that is the primary draw today, luring people from all over the world to the city by the Mississippi. This was not the case in 1953. Vernon and Gladys Presley weren't thinking about blues or gospel music that year, and the term "rock 'n' roll" was years away from being coined. To a struggling family from the Mississippi Delta, the main appeal of Memphis was that, economically, it was not the dead end that poverty-stricken Tupelo, Mississippi, had become for them. Memphis was a postwar promised land, with factories, hotels, stores, affordable housing, and a climate of innovation and hope for the future. It was "the big city," a place to better oneself, get some regular work, find a decent place to live, and raise a child to go to church and to school. The Presleys believed that, for their son, Memphis was the place to make dreams come true.

They had no idea how right they were.

Elvis, age twelve. This photograph was taken about a year before the Presleys
moved from Tupelo, Mississippi, to Memphis.

chapter 2

the boy from tupelo

On any evening in the mid-twentieth century, downtown Memphis was like a snapshot of urban Middle America with a distinctively Southern flavor, genteel affluence juxtaposed with working-class grit. On one end of Main Street, the city's commercial hub, a gentleman in a seersucker suit might be squiring his lady to a night on the town, perhaps to a dance at the Peabody Skyway. Down the street, a farmer in denim overalls might be enjoying a beer after a day in the cotton fields, sitting next to a couple of laborers weary from working at factories near the Memphis & Arkansas Bridge. In the humid air, a breeze might waft in from the mighty Mississippi, and a visitor might catch a scent of succulent smoke from one of the city's famous barbecue joints.

Some black faces were scattered among white ones, although the blacks on Main Street were usually at work in barbershops, shoeshine stands, and hotel lobbies. After dark, many would head south to Beale Street, the acknowledged border between white and black Memphis. A few curious white youths who either ignored or simply had not yet learned the long-held prejudices of their elders might also head down to Beale to listen to music and soak in a culture that was somehow both intimately familiar yet entirely alien.

Hardly anyone in Memphis took notice when a family from East Tupelo, Mississippi, moved into the rooming house at

(1) 370 Washington Street on November 6, 1948. The Presleys were something of an odd couple: Vernon was handsome but dour and taciturn; his wife, the former Gladys Love Smith, was extroverted, personable, and bubbly. Gladys doted on the couple's only child, Elvis Aaron, born on January 8, 1935. Elvis was actually a twin; his brother, named Jesse Garon, died stillborn, a misfortune that haunted the surviving brother throughout his life.

Vernon had been briefly jailed in Tupelo in 1938 for check forgery; after he was released, the Presleys moved around as Vernon sought work doing odd jobs such as house painting and truck driving. The family often relied on the kindness and hospitality of relatives for lodging and employment. They never really set down roots until Elvis, his mother, and his father arrived in Memphis—just another poor family from the sticks, settling into one of the mid-South's most dynamic cities, looking for an opportunity to better their fortunes. The Presleys quietly moved the following year to **(2) 572 Poplar Avenue**, a big Victorian house that had been subdivided into single-room apartments. Vernon paid around $10 a week to rent one of those tiny rooms.

If Memphians had a crystal ball and could foresee the legendary figure that Elvis would become, perhaps they might have made an effort to preserve his earliest homes. Unfortunately, no trace remains of the Presley family's first two residences in Memphis. The Washington Street building was demolished; the site is now an empty lot surrounded by a chain-link fence. The Poplar Street house is also gone, replaced by a parking lot.

making a living

Vernon soon got a job at the Precision Tool Company. The company, which manufactured munitions, also hired Gladys's brother Travis, who had moved nearby with his wife, Lorraine. Gladys found work at a company called Fashion Curtains as a sewing machine operator, and later at St. Joseph's Hospital, 220 Overton Avenue. Erected in

1885 and operated by the Catholic Sisters of St. Francis, St. Joseph's merged with another hospital, Baptist Memorial Health Care, in 1997. The St. Joseph's buildings and property were sold to nearby St. Jude's Children's Research Hospital, which demolished most of the original buildings for an expansion. St. Jude's translational trials unit, originally built as an emergency room annex, is the last trace of the old St. Joseph's complex. (The original St. Joseph's is where Dr. Martin Luther King, Jr., was pronounced dead on April 4, 1968.)

Even with both parents working, the Presleys struggled to get by. Vernon, who throughout his life was regarded as fairly unambitious and unmotivated and suffered from a bad back, tended to change jobs often. In the spring of 1949, he became a loader at the United Paint Company, at Third Street and Auction Avenue, a site now also taken over by St. Jude's. With the main breadwinner taking home about $40 a week, the family applied for public assistance and was granted admission to the **(3) Lauderdale Courts** on September 20, 1949.

The Courts, as they were known, were situated on twenty-two acres in downtown Memphis encompassing sixty-six red-brick buildings. The Presleys' apartment, at 185 Winchester Avenue, was a definite upgrade from their previous homes. For about $35 a month, the family got a living room, two bedrooms, a kitchen, and their own bathroom (on Poplar, they had to share one with the other tenants). The apartment was also closer to Vernon's job, and it was just a few blocks away from Elvis's favorite hangouts, such as Poplar Tunes and Charlie's Records, which fed his ravenous appetite for new music, and the Suzore No. 2 theater, where he whiled away many lazy afternoons watching movies. The Courts were also a short stroll from gospel sing-alongs at Ellis Auditorium and the blues clubs of Beale Street.

Lauderdale Courts was the first housing project built in Memphis and one of the first in the United States. It was erected in 1938 under the auspices of President Franklin Delano Roosevelt's Works Progress Administration (WPA) program, replacing a collection of run-down shacks. Memphis's top architects at the time—J. Frazer Smith, Walk C. Jones, Sr., George Awsumb, Edwin B. Phillips, and several others—pooled their talents to design a complex that would foster a sense of community. The buildings were designed in a colonial revival style, with brick exteriors, art moderne metal newel posts, and metal porch roofs with ornamental supports. Surrounding the buildings were landscaped courtyards and the Market Mall, a grassy communal space where Elvis would one day play guitar for his neighbors. Inside the apartments were oak parquet floors and indoor bathrooms (a luxury for poor families at the time).

The Presleys arrived with few possessions of their own to an apartment that wasn't quite ready for them. The walls needed a paint job, the blinds in one bedroom were broken, the bathroom sink was stopped up, and the oven door would not shut properly. After the fixes were made, however, the family settled into their new home nicely; according to the inspectors who checked up on the residents' homes, Gladys was an excellent housekeeper.

Elvis's bedroom window faced Third Street, and some former neighbors recall seeing him strumming his guitar while sitting at the windowsill. He would also hang out in the laundry room in the basement, practicing his guitar skills.

saving the courts

Lauderdale Courts provided a solid foundation that helped lift many of its residents out of poverty, but by the 1980s and 1990s, conditions had deteriorated to the point where only 75 of the nearly 500 apartments in the complex were occupied, and the buildings were scheduled for demolition. When the general public got wind of the fact that Elvis's childhood home was facing the wrecking ball, thanks to an article in the *New York Times*, a coalition comprising Elvis fans and the preservationist group Memphis Heritage joined forces to save Lauderdale Courts, raising funds and petitioning the mayor and the U.S. secretary of housing and urban development to add Lauderdale Courts to the National Register of Historic Places.

The Courts' new landmark status could not stave off the inevitable, however; with deteriorating conditions and a shrinking tenant base, it closed in 2000. The Memphis Housing Authority hired developers to renovate the complex so it could serve as a mixed-income housing site, spending $36 million over four years. Now renamed Uptown Square, it is home to upper-middle-class professionals as well as families on public assistance and was Memphis's first wireless community.

Best of all for Elvis fans, unlike the Poplar Street and Washington Street homes, the Presleys' Lauderdale Courts apartment, #328, now called the Presley Apartment, was preserved and is open year-round to visitors who wish to stay in Elvis's old room. (Aside from Graceland, Elvis lived here longer than in any of his other Memphis homes.) The apartment is furnished with vintage furniture and fixtures, including a working refrigerator from 1951, alongside modern conveniences such as a plasma HDTV and a microwave oven. Some items in Elvis's old bedroom have been faithfully restored. On the dresser are a replica of the *Humes High Herald* yearbook from 1953 and a jar of Elvis's favorite hair care product, Royal Crown Hair Dressing; on the walls are photos of his favorite movie stars, Tony Curtis and Rudolph Valentino. Visitors can sit on the large, sixteen-inch-deep windowsill where Elvis used to practice his guitar.

The apartment is unavailable for stays only twice a year: during Elvis's birthday week in January and during Elvis Week, which commemorates his death, in August. During these times, visitors can tour the apartment for a modest fee.

school ties

The same year the Presley family moved into Lauderdale Courts, Elvis began his freshman year at **(4) L. C. Humes High School**, today called Humes Middle School.

Opened in the 1930s, Humes High School, at 695 North Manassas Street at the end of Jackson Avenue, is now listed on the

National Register of Historic Places due to its connection to Elvis Presley. Not only would Elvis play his first real performances there, but he would also forge bonds with people who would remain in his circle for the rest of his life. First, however, Elvis had to come out of his shell; after tiny Tupelo, he had found Memphis a bit frightening.

Elvis clearly was different from his classmates. He loved to dress up like the "colored folk" on Beale Street, wearing flashy clothing—black satin pants with pink stripes, shirts with turned-up collars—and meticulously styling his thick black hair into a ducktail with a front curl. What the other students didn't know about, at least not at first, was their classmate's passion for music and singing, which his natural shyness caused him to keep hidden. Elvis had always loved music. Back in Tupelo, he won a singing contest at a local fair at the age of eight, performing the maudlin country-and-western ballad "Old Shep" by Red Foley. For his eleventh birthday, his mother gave him a gift that he treasured for years: a little guitar purchased from the Tupelo Hardware Company. This said less about her early recognition of his talent than it did about the Presleys' woeful economic condition: the guitar was cheaper than the bicycle that Elvis had requested.

His shyness, along with his offbeat fashion sense, a stuttering problem, and his dirt-poor background, made it hard for Elvis to make friends at Humes; it didn't help that his mom, according to his cousin Billy Smith, walked him to school well into his teens. Acquaintances from his high school days recall Elvis being picked on and ostracized. He had few male friends, but even back then he had a way with girls, who were drawn to his smoldering good looks, chivalrous manners, and emotional vulnerability. His female friends far outnumbered his male ones.

One of those male friends was all-Memphis football star Red West, another kid from a poor family. Elvis loved football and decided to try out for the high school team. One day after practice, other boys from the team cornered Elvis in a restroom and threatened to cut his hair. Red intervened to protect him; from that point on, Red was a guardian to Elvis, forging a relationship that would last through much of the two men's lives despite the fact that Elvis was cut from the team because he refused to heed the coach's demand that he cut his hair. (Elvis's love of the sport persisted, however; as an adult, he often played touch football with friends and business associates to unwind.)

Elvis also made friends with the eventual senior class president, George Klein, one of the few students in the "in" crowd who gave him the time of day. They met in Miss Marman's music appreciation class in 1948 and remained friends until graduation. Klein attended Memphis State University on his way to a career in radio that would bring him back into Elvis's life. In fact, both Red West and George Klein became members of the "Memphis Mafia," the entourage of friends and hangers-on that surrounded Elvis at the height of his fame. Elvis joined the ROTC program and became a voracious reader of books—history and literature especially, as well as Captain Marvel comic books. Elvis idolized the superhero with the lightning-bolt emblem, who was transformed from a boy into an adult hero just by uttering "Shazam!"

As a student, Elvis was average to decent, getting a few As, some Bs, and—in eighth grade—a C in music. Told by a music teacher that he couldn't sing, Elvis brought his guitar to class and belted out a 1947 hit called "Keep Them Cold Icy Fingers off of Me" to prove the teacher wrong.

His musical gifts did not stay hidden from his fellow students for long. When he was sixteen, Elvis began taking guitar lessons from Jesse Lee Denson, the son of a local minister. The better he got at music, the more self-confident he became. On the evening of April 9, 1953, the school held its annual talent show. Elvis was coaxed into performing; but he told only a handful of his friends that he was going to do it. That night, there was no trace of the natural stage presence for which Elvis would later become famous: he appeared awkward and out of sorts when he first came on stage, but when he started singing his first number, Teresa Brewer's "Till I Waltz Again with You," the audience was transfixed. Most had no idea Elvis could sing. This evening is regarded as the first time Elvis performed for a large audience.

Humes, an all-white school when Elvis attended, closed as a high school in 1967. It later reopened as an integrated preparatory middle school, with a mission of turning out young scholars. Its modern dress code, which requires uniforms, would not have thrilled Elvis. Today, Humes is a regular stop on Elvis-focused tours of Memphis, even though the neighborhood around the school, like several sections of Memphis outside of the restored downtown, is somewhat blighted.

ushering in a career

Elvis was determined to pitch in financially to help out his mother and father, who still struggled to get by even with public assistance. His first job, in the summer after his sophomore year, was as an usher at the **(5) Loew's State Theatre**, 152 South Main Street, one of several grand theaters that dotted Memphis's main thoroughfare during the golden age of cinema, only a few of which have been preserved.

Loew's State Theatre was built in 1925, converted from a warehouse that faced Second Street. The owners desired the more prestigious Main Street address aligned with the Second Street building, so they purchased the storefront to expand the theater. Unfortunately, there was an alley separating the two structures that the city would not let the owners close off by connecting them. The novel solution was to gut the Main Street storefront and use it as a vast, ornate, half-block-long lobby leading to a grand staircase. The staircase connected to a bridge that led patrons over the alley and into the balcony-level seating.

Loew's State Theatre was built at the same time as its sister theater, the Loews Palace on Union Avenue. Both originally served as vaudeville theaters, with a large pit and stage and a Wurlitzer organ. Both were designed in the neoclassical Adamesque style used by architect Thomas Lamb, who employed classical Roman decorative motifs such as framed medallions, vases, urns, sphinxes, griffins, and vine scrolls; painted ornaments; and ornate pastel color schemes.

In 1964, the Loews Corporation sold the theater to another chain, Gulf State Theaters, which owned and operated the venue for six years. The marquee in those last years of its existence was somewhat awkward looking, as the new owners covered and painted over the Loews logo, leaving only the slightly off-center word "Theatre." The Loew's State Theatre closed down in 1970; the last movie shown there was *WUSA*, a movie starring Paul Newman.

Elvis's gig at the Loew's State Theatre didn't last long. He was fired after getting into a fight with another employee. He then took a job with Vernon's old employer, Precision Tool, where he made $27 a week working on the assembly line. However, this job was also relatively short-lived. Perhaps because of Elvis's well-known run-in with the high school football team, stories have cropped up claiming that his refusal to cut his hair was the reason for getting fired from Precision Tool. In reality, Elvis was let go simply because he was under age; he lied about his age when he applied for the job.

During his senior year, Elvis took a job at MARL Metal Products, a furniture-manufacturing company located near the Memphis & Arkansas Bridge. A day or so after graduation, he started work at M. B. Parker's Machinist Shop. The last job Elvis held before his meteoric musical career took off was at **(6) Crown Electric**, whose offices were located at Poplar Avenue and what is today called Danny Thomas Boulevard. Elvis trained as an electrician's apprentice and drove a truck. (Among the many items of Elvis-themed apparel that visitors can purchase in the gift shops of Graceland, one of the best for "in-the-know" Elvis mavens is a replica Crown Electric work shirt.)

Clearly, Elvis had a strong work ethic from a young age and felt a sense of responsibility to provide for his family. But he didn't have much real enthusiasm for the working life. It seems the only career he was suited for was a musical one. His desire always was to make music, to use his flair for singing and showmanship to lift his family from poverty; all he needed was for someone to give him a chance.

the home of the blues

One aspect of Lauderdale Courts that appealed to Elvis was its proximity to Beale Street, whose place in the history of music—and in Elvis's formative musical education—is hard to overstate. Beale Street brought the blues to America.

The street—known as Beale Avenue until the popularity of W. C. Handy's "Beale Street Blues" inspired the city to rename it—was established in 1841 by developer Robertson Topp, who named it after a military hero about whom little is known. The street runs from East Street in downtown Memphis all the way to the Mississippi River. At the western end, near the river, were saloons, warehouses, and brothels; between Main and Third Street were retail shops and other respectable businesses; and east of Third Street was an affluent suburb, populated by plantation owners in grand mansions. Beale Street began to develop its modern identity as a musical hub in the 1860s, when black musicians flocked there to perform. Among the first was Sam Thomas's Young Men's Brass Band, which began performing there around 1860.

In the aftermath of the yellow fever epidemics in the 1870s and the subsequent bankruptcy of the city of Memphis, Robert Church purchased land around Beale Street and spearheaded efforts to revitalize it, even paying the city to create a community space, called Church Park, at the corner of Fourth and Beale in 1899. Church became the South's first black millionaire partly due to his investments on Beale Street, and he inspired other blacks with entrepreneurial spirit to open businesses there. Many of these businesses—some legitimate, such as restaurants and retail stores; others less so, such as gambling dens—took advantage of what was becoming the area's most valuable resource: the abundance of talented black musicians who were drawn to Beale Street.

Because of the Jim Crow laws that segregated the city parks at the time, Church Park became a gathering spot for the African American community. Many of the blues musicians who later performed in Beale

Street nightclubs first played for crowds at Church Park. Its auditorium, with room for two thousand people, also hosted such historic speakers as Booker T. Washington and presidents Woodrow Wilson and Franklin D. Roosevelt.

The early twentieth century saw the rise of black-owned clubs and restaurants on Beale. The oldest surviving African American church, Beale Street Baptist Church, was erected in 1864 and played a role in the civil rights movement of the 1960s. Ida Wells, a cofounder of the National Association for the Advancement of Colored People (NAACP), ran the anti-segregationist newspaper *Free Speech* from an office on Beale starting in 1889.

In 1905, W. C. Handy—then a trumpet player in Clarksdale, Mississippi—arrived, invited by Memphis mayor Thornton to be a music instructor for his Knights of Pythias band. Handy and his song "Memphis Blues" paved the way for the genre-defining artists who followed, including a young man from Indianola, Mississippi, named Riley King, who arrived, guitar in tow, in 1946. King, who had grown up singing in a gospel choir, became a singing DJ for the pioneering all-black radio station WDIA and acquired the nickname "Beale Street Blues Boy," which was shortened to "B. B."

By the time B. B. King arrived, Beale Street was a prime blues destination. The unique music scene had blossomed in the decades between the world wars. The legends of rhythm and blues who preceded King on Beale Street included Louis Armstrong, Muddy Waters, Memphis Minnie McCoy, Alberta Hunter, Albert King, Furry Lewis, and Rufus Thomas.

healing beale

During the 1950s, Beale Street's music and cultural scene was an irresistible magnet for Elvis Presley. He often crossed the border at the corner of Beale and Main into the "colored section" and strolled down Beale, sometimes popping into the clubs to hear musicians and to check out the local fashions. Despite his skin color, he felt a kinship with the denizens of Beale. Like them, he loved blues harmonies and slick clothing, and he had the hopeful striving that all poor dreamers share.

In the 1960s, years of postwar economic decline began to take their toll on Beale Street. The urban renewal projects of the 1970s resulted in many of the clubs and shops being boarded up. Despite the decay, however, Beale Street was eventually recognized for its contributions to American music. The section of the street between Main and Fourth Streets was declared a National Historic Landmark on May 23, 1966; an act of Congress on December 15, 1977, officially proclaimed Beale Street as the "Home of the Blues." None of these honors, however, could stop the deterioration of this once-prosperous boulevard; at one point, virtually every building in the historic district was boarded up except for A. Schwab's Dry Goods Store, the only business in continuous operation from its founding until the present day.

In 1973, George B. Miller founded the Beale Street Development Corporation. Miller teamed with boxer Muhammad Ali to open the Muhammad Ali Theatre in 1979 in an effort to bring more business to the area.

In 1982, the city leased the designated Beale Street Historic District, from Second to Fourth Avenues, to Miller's company for $10 million in federal grants. A year later, developer John Elkington, whose company, Elkington & Keltner, was responsible for maintaining the sidewalks, streets, and other common areas of the district, paid a visit there and was distressed by how little progress had been made: Beale was still a virtual ghost town, with fenced-in streets and boarded-up storefronts. Elkington convinced the city to sell the historic district to him. Elkington's efforts to bring big-time commerce and tourism dollars back to the heart of Beale Street were an unqualified success.

The Beale Street of today is a hopping, lively destination for visitors looking to hear some blues and visit some cultural landmarks. However, much like Bourbon Street in New Orleans or Times Square in New York, its status as a tourist hub has washed away much of the authentic grit of its earlier days. It is now the largest tourist attraction in all of Tennessee, outpacing Graceland and even Nashville's Grand Ole Opry, drawing more than 4.2 million visitors annually and responsible for more than seven hundred jobs and over $30 million a year in revenue.

What remains on the revitalized Beale Street that has a link to Elvis? Not much. The **(7) Blues City Café**, 138 Beale at Second Street, stands at the site of Nathan Novick's old pawnshop, where, according to local legend, Elvis (as well as other Memphis musicians) shopped for secondhand guitars. Today, the old building is one of the street's many live-music destinations, as well as the headquarters of Backbeat Tours, which offers bus tours around the city with narration accompanied by music from local musicians.

A movie house called the Malco Theatre in Elvis's time, the **(8) Orpheum Theatre for the Performing Arts**, 203 South Main Street at Beale Street, includes space that once served as a barbershop. According to local legend, Elvis got his hair cut there. Elvis worked at the Malco for a time after getting fired from Loew's State Theatre.

At 126 Beale Street is a nightclub called Republic. At one time, this location housed an establishment called Elvis Presley's Memphis, a tourist-friendly restaurant and nightclub that opened after Elvis's death. Elvis obviously never ate at this eatery or set foot in the nightspot that replaced it, but the nightclub did take over the location of a place that Elvis did frequent throughout his life—the store that sold him his first suit—and his last.

clothes fit for a king

More than music lured Elvis to Beale Street. Anyone who remembers the increasingly flamboyant stage costumes of the King of Rock 'n' Roll would not be surprised to discover that Elvis's predilection for flashy garments began early in his life.

By the 1950s, **(9) Lansky Brothers Clothiers**, a fixture of the African American community at its original location at 126 Beale Street, was famous throughout Memphis for its dapper, avant-garde apparel. Founders Bernard and Guy Lansky were two of nine children, the sons of immigrants from Kiev. (One of their relatives—according to some sources—was Meyer Lansky, the infamous organized crime figure.) Their father bought the store where the two brothers set up shop in 1946, originally as an Army-Navy surplus store selling used World War II apparel and items. As the Beale Street music scene flourished in the late 1940s—bringing black performers looking to up their style quotient and fans who wanted to emulate them—Bernard saw a niche that needed to be filled.

Lansky's catered to the neighborhood that surrounded it in the 1950s—populated increasingly by pimps, gamblers, and musicians who frequented Beale's clubs, restaurants, bars, and dope dens. Lansky stocked the shop with mohair and sharkskin suits with short-waisted jackets, plaid tuxedo jackets, peg-leg pants with flared legs and no back pockets, bolero jackets, and "Hi-Boy" shirts with short, rolled collars and three-inch cuffs, a variation of the style popularized by trumpet player Billy Eckstine, inventor of the "Mr. B" shirt. Lansky's fashions were what today some would call "ghetto fabulous." They may owe some of their popularity to practicality: lightweight mohair suits were more comfortable than wool in Memphis's hot, humid subtropical climate. Temperatures regularly reach into the 90s during the summer, with hot, dry weather coming up from Texas and humidity blowing in from the Gulf of Mexico. Such garments were also ideal for musicians and other entertainers who sweat under the lights onstage.

Elvis Presley started coming in around 1952, staring longingly at Lansky's window displays. Bernard Lansky recalls Elvis telling him, "You have some nice stuff here. When I get rich, I'll buy you out." Lansky replied, "Don't buy me out; just buy from me." Thus a lifelong relationship was born. Elvis's first purchase from Lansky's was a shirt for $3.95, bought after the young man cashed a paycheck from his job at the Loew's State Theatre. Shortly thereafter, Elvis ordered a custom-tailored tuxedo for his senior prom: black pants, pink jacket, and pink-and-black cummerbund. Elvis, Lansky recalls, was always partial to black suits with pink piping, and the color combo is still used on much Elvis-related merchandise.

Elvis also came to Lansky to get outfitted for his first appearance on the *Ed Sullivan Show* in 1956. Because Elvis was not making big money, Lansky gave him the suit on credit. As Elvis's fame grew and his distinctive look became more and more coveted by performers, Lansky's shop on Beale Street became a destination for people from around the country. With musicians such as B. B. King, Count Basie, Duke Ellington, Otis Redding, Jerry Lee Lewis, Ace Cannon, Roy Orbison, the Temptations, Frank Sinatra, Carl Perkins, and others as customers, Lansky became the unofficial tailor to musical royalty. "Elvis was my PR man all over the world," Lansky once told an interviewer. Another Memphis-based musician who went on to worldwide fame, Johnny Cash, once came in with a can of Price Albert tobacco, pointed to the character on the can, and said, "I want this." The black suit with cutaway coat that Lansky created kicked off Cash's iconic "man in black" look.

Even Lansky's could not survive Beale Street's economic woes in the 1960s and 1970s, however. The store moved to its current location in the ornate grand lobby of the Peabody Hotel in 1981. Bernard bought out his brother Guy shortly thereafter and now runs the store with his son, Hal. (Actually, there are now four Lansky-branded stores on the Peabody lobby floor, selling gifts and sundries in addition to apparel.) Lansky wisely held onto the property that housed the original Beale Street store.

peabody memories

In addition to being the modern-day location of Lansky Brothers, the **(10) Peabody Hotel**, 149 Union Avenue at Second Street, was the stage for several other significant events in Elvis Presley's early life. The hotel's Continental Ballroom was the site of his senior prom in

1953. Elvis's date that night was a freshman at the Holy Names School named Regis Vaughan, whom he had met at Lauderdale Courts, where she lived with her mother. Elvis and Regis dated for several months, often double-dating with Elvis's cousin Gene Smith and his girlfriend. For prom, Elvis wore a shiny new blue suit purchased at Lansky's. Even though he had become comfortable singing in public, he was still embarrassed about his dancing, so the couple spent their time together sitting around sipping Cokes. That evening, Elvis joined a long list of luminaries who have set foot in the Peabody, the grande dame of the mid-South, since it was built in 1869.

"The Mississippi Delta begins in the lobby of the Peabody Hotel," wrote essayist David Cohn in 1935. "If you stand near its fountain in the middle of the lobby . . . ultimately you will see everybody who is anybody in the Delta." This is just as true today.

The original Peabody, on the corner of Main Street and Monroe Avenue, was built by Robert Campbell Brinkley, who named it for his friend George Foster Peabody, a philanthropist who had died shortly before the building was completed. The hotel hosted General Robert E. Lee, President Andrew Johnson, and three generations of Romanovs—the czars of Russia—along with numerous cotton traders, railroad magnates, and Southern socialites. It also served as a temporary home for the former president of the Confederacy, Jefferson Davis, in 1870.

The Peabody's successful early years gave way to hard times beginning with the Panic of 1873, which hammered the stock market and was responsible for business failures, home foreclosures, and massive unemployment nationwide. The devastating yellow fever epidemics of the 1870s made a bad situation worse, rendering Memphis a virtual ghost town. The hotel endured, however, sheltering victims of the fever and closing only briefly; it reopened in 1879, and by the time the city of Memphis regained its city charter in 1893, the Peabody had reestablished itself as the city's grand hotel. As the new century began, however, more problems loomed, such as increased competition from new, more modern hotels and the onset of World War I.

The structure was torn down in 1923. The current Peabody Hotel, opened in 1925, was erected a few blocks away, on the site of the old Fransioli Hotel (which had a very similar décor). Designed in the Italian Renaissance style by Chicago architect Walter W. Altschlager, the Peabody featured a huge two-story lobby with a mezzanine balcony supported by massive square columns. The centerpiece of the lobby was a beautiful fountain made of black Italian travertine marble. The new Peabody was an unqualified success, and its grand lobby became "Memphis's living room."

In 1965, it was sold to the Sheraton hotel chain, which catered to business travelers and conventioneers and tried to give the rooms a more contemporary look. Like many other historic buildings in Memphis, the Peabody fell victim to economic woes and urban blight in the 1970s—at one point, squatters took up residence in abandoned rooms—and closed in 1973. It got a new lease on life in 1975, when the family of Memphis entrepreneur Jack Belz purchased the property and initiated a $25 million renovation. The hotel's reopening, which is widely regarded as providing a key stimulus for downtown Memphis's revitalization, took place on September 1, 1981.

a grand revival

The modern twelve-story Peabody Hotel has more than four hundred guest rooms, including a presidential suite where numerous U.S. presidents have stayed. It has ballrooms and conference rooms, gift shops and restaurants, and an antique piano once owned by Francis Scott Key, who wrote the words to "The Star-Spangled Banner." The bustling lobby is dominated by the ornate marble fountain and is especially popular during the afternoon, when ducks splash around in the fountain for the enjoyment of the crowds.

On the hotel's rooftop is the Skyway, a ballroom that has long been a favorite spot for dining, dancing, and moonlit romance. With a huge beechwood dance floor and the capacity to seat hundreds of guests, the Skyway has hosted countless banquets, weddings, birthday and graduation parties, and high-society events.

Like nearly every other significant building in Memphis, the Peabody played a role in the city's musical evolution. In the 1930s and 1940s, the Skyway was the site of regular radio broadcasts. Memphis station WREC broadcast musical performances from there, and CBS picked them up in 1937 to send out to a national audience. In its heyday, the broadcast featured the greats of the big band era—Glenn Miller, Tommy Dorsey, Harry James, Clyde McCoy, the Andrews Sisters.

In the 1950s, WREC was the broadcaster of radio programs such as *Meet Kitty Kelly* and *Treasury Bandstand*, many of which were written, directed, and produced by a woman who would play an important role in the development of Elvis Presley's musical career: Marion Keisker. The basement of the Peabody housed WREC's headquarters, and it was there that Keisker first met Sun Records founder Sam Phillips, who also worked as a radio engineer for the Skyway broadcasts. This meeting would have great significance for Elvis and the nascent musical genre that would come to be known as rock 'n' roll.

♫♫♫♫

by the way

the peabody duck march

A visit to the Peabody Hotel would be incomplete without a glimpse of the ducks, the hotel's most famous residents. Every morning at eleven, led by the hotel's "Duckmaster," half a dozen mallards emerge from an elevator in the lobby and march down a red carpet to the accompaniment of John Philip Sousa's "King Cotton March" on their way to the fountain. There they stay until five in the afternoon, when the Duckmaster leads the procession back to the elevator and to the waterfowl's home in the "Duck Palace" on the hotel roof. The Duck March, as it has become known, draws observers from far and wide, often lined up three deep along the red carpet with cameras to record the daily pilgrimage. The onslaught of paparazzi as the ducks make their stroll reminds one of the celebrity red carpet arrivals on Oscar night.

This odd but much-beloved tradition started in 1932, when Peabody general manager Frank Schutt and a friend returned from a duck-hunting trip empty-handed and drunk from too much Tennessee whiskey. As a prank, they decided to put their decoys—which were live ducks—in the hotel fountain before heading off to bed. Schutt woke the next morning with only a hazy memory of his antics the night before but soon noticed that guests were gathered around the fountain, delighted by the ducks.

Schutt knew a genuine attraction when he saw one. He hired Edward Pembrok, formerly an animal tamer from the Barnum & Bailey circus, to train a trio of mallards to perform the now-familiar ritual march in unison. This choreographed version of the duck march became a trademark of the hotel. When the Peabody reopened in 1981, it reinstated the beloved tradition.

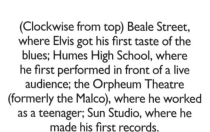

(Clockwise from top) Beale Street, where Elvis got his first taste of the blues; Humes High School, where he first performed in front of a live audience; the Orpheum Theatre (formerly the Malco), where he worked as a teenager; Sun Studio, where he made his first records.

chapter 3

rising star

Things began to happen fast for Elvis Presley after he graduated from Humes High School in 1953. By this time, the Presleys had changed residences again. They were forced to move out of Lauderdale Courts in January 1953 because the family's income—with both Gladys and Elvis working to supplement Vernon's paychecks—exceeded the maximum allowed by the Memphis Housing Authority.

The day before Elvis's eighteenth birthday, January 7, 1953, the family moved into a rooming house at **(11) 698 Saffarans Street** (now an empty lot). It was only a few blocks from Humes High but was smaller and more expensive than their apartment at the Courts. The Presleys felt as though they had taken a step back down the ladder; once again they had to share a bathroom with other tenants. Fortunately, they stayed for only a few months. In April, they moved to an old Victorian on 462 Alabama Street (now a stretch of interstate) that had been split into two large apartments. The Presleys lived in the bottom-floor apartment for the next year and a half.

Elvis settled into some habits and hangouts. He was driving a truck for Crown Electric, listening to the blues musicians on Beale Street, and hanging out at record stores such as Charlie's, Henry's, and Poplar Tunes with his friends. Near Charlie's was the Suzore No. 2 theater, where Elvis often took dates.

Music was already a big business in Memphis when Elvis arrived, whether recording, selling, broadcasting, or, in the case of Lansky Brothers, dressing it up. By the 1950s, Memphis had become a hotbed of musical innovation and a magnet to hopeful musicians of all types. What made Memphis unique among American cities with a musical tradition was its diversity. To the east, Nashville was the acknowledged epicenter of commercial country-and-western music, but its sound mostly followed a formula, one in which any "black music" influences were weeded out. Artists influenced by blues, gospel, or other regional styles rarely found an audience there. To the south, New Orleans was insular in its love of black genres and mostly only black artists; white singers specializing in country or pop were not successful there. Memphis embraced the disparate genres and was the first to meld them together. The diversity in musical styles was reflected in Memphis's radio stations and on the shelves of its music stores; Elvis loved them all.

a matter of records

Of the record stores that Elvis patronized, the one that had the biggest impact on him—and the only one of which any trace remains in modern-day Memphis—is **(12) Poplar Tunes**, 308 Poplar Avenue, within easy walking distance of Lauderdale Courts. Also called Pop Tunes, it was founded in 1946 by Joe Cuoghi and John Novarese. The store became known as the place for teens to find the newest hit records, many of which were first played by Memphis disc jockey Dewey Phillips on his influential radio show *Red Hot and Blue*. The store's success—some of which may have been due to its then-unusual policy of allowing customers to listen to records before buying them—led Cuoghi to found his own Memphis-based record label, Hi Records, in 1957. Hi Records would become Memphis's premier hit factory for soul recordings in the 1970s, releasing chart-toppers from artists such as Al Green.

Elvis continued to visit Pop Tunes even after he hit it big, often coming in to see how his records were selling. Cuoghi's brother Vince recalled in an interview that Elvis was painfully shy and would hide in a corner of the shop when he noticed a patron purchasing one of his discs.

Poplar Tunes opened a second store in the 1990s. In 2001, both stores were acquired by Nashville-based Music City Record Distributors. But like so many other small record shops, they fell victim to the proliferation of big-box retailers and the advent of digital, downloadable music. Both closed their doors in 2009, and Memphis music lovers continue to lament their passing. After standing empty for a time, the original Poplar Tunes building became a Chinese restaurant.

Visitors to the city can see the iconic neon sign that stood for years outside the original Poplar Avenue store, thanks to Memphis clothier Hal Lansky. He bought the sign and donated it to the (13) **Memphis Rock and Soul Museum**, located at 191 Beale Street at Highway 61, inside the FedEx Forum sports arena. The Smithsonian Institution established the museum initially as a traveling exhibit in 1996; the permanent site in Memphis's premier sports venue opened in 2004. The Pop Tunes sign is one of numerous artifacts there that remind visitors of the impact that Memphis's musical genres have had on American culture.

memphis's biggest stage

The Humes High School graduating class of 1953 had its commencement ceremony in the South Hall of (14) **Ellis Auditorium**, a huge multipurpose arena built in the 1920s at the intersection of Poplar Avenue and Front Street. Originally called the Memphis and Shelby County Auditorium and Market House, and renamed for manager Robert R. Ellis in 1930, it was designed by architect Carl Awsumb in the Italian Renaissance style. The auditorium functioned as a concert hall, athletic arena, convention center, and produce market; the builders who financed the auditorium were skeptical that entertainment revenue alone would allow them to recoup their investment, and insisted on the produce market to ensure that they made some money. But it's not as though the auditorium organizers did not try for—and, in many cases, get—some of the biggest names in the business. The program for the auditorium's opening night featured legendary bandleader John Philip Sousa; others who performed there over the years included Guy Lombardo, Paul Whiteman, B. B. King, and Ray Charles.

Ellis Auditorium was divided into two halls. Musical acts, ice shows, sporting events, circuses, and other live events were staged in the expansive North Hall, while movies and stage plays took place in the smaller South Hall. The two halls were divided by a stage, which had an elevator that enabled dramatic entrances from beneath. Massive curtains could be opened so that both halls could be used at once.

The auditorium had a separate side entrance for black patrons and a separate balcony in which they were seated, standard arrangements at the time in Memphis and the rest of the segregated South. The most popular sporting events were basketball games; despite the racial divide that persisted in the city throughout the 1950s and 1960s, six thousand white patrons paid to see the all-black Harlem Globetrotters play there in 1953. Pro wrestling, or "rasslin'," featuring headliners such as Gorgeous George, was also a big draw there for many years.

Elvis, with his first band, guitarist Scotty Moore and bassist Bill Black, would perform several shows at Ellis Auditorium. On February 6, 1955, they were one of the acts in the Five Star Jamboree concert, which featured contemporary country hit makers like Faron Young and Ferlin Husky. In 1956, Elvis headlined the Cotton Pickin' Jamboree, the opening-night concert for Memphis's annual Cotton Carnival, along with the Jordanaires and country singer Hank Snow.

Ellis Auditorium was razed in 1999 to expand the space of the Memphis Cook Convention Center next door. In 2003, the Cannon Center for the Performing Arts, home of the Memphis Symphony Orchestra, opened its doors on the site of the former Ellis Auditorium.

the cradle of rock

Much has been written about the day that Elvis Presley walked into (15) **Sun Studio** at 706 Union Avenue, today regarded as a shrine for lovers of rock 'n' roll history. It was the summer of 1953, and the legend that persists is that the shy Elvis planned to make a record to give to his mother for her birthday. Other sources say that Elvis just wanted to know how his voice would sound on a record (Gladys Presley's birthday was in the spring). Still others point out that Elvis could have gone to any small studio to get his voice on tape, but he had stardom on his mind, and the fact that Sun had already gained a reputation for taking chances on unproven talent and achieving success—as it had recently with a group Elvis liked, called the Prisonaires, a quintet of singing convicts, and their song, "Just Walkin' in the Rain"—gave the young man hope.

Sun Records founder Sam Phillips had established the Memphis Recording Service (as it was then known) in January 1950. The youngest of eight children, raised on a farm in Florence, Alabama, Phillips saw his family lose much of its savings in the crash of 1929; after his father died in 1941, eighteen-year-old Phillips went to work at a series of odd jobs to support the family. He eventually moved into radio broadcasting, working at various stations throughout the mid-South and ultimately landing at Memphis's WREC, which had its offices in the basement of the Peabody Hotel. There he met Marion Keisker, who would become his assistant.

When Phillips opened his recording studio, his business agenda was clear: he was interested in discovering and recording new musical talent, with a particular focus on the many talented black artists who were emerging in Memphis. He was convinced that there was a regional, if not national, market for this music. But he also kept an open mind about what the next big hit might be: the Memphis Recording Service's motto was "We record anyone, anytime, anywhere."

The studio has a unique place in music history, having made what most consider the first rock 'n' roll recording (in large part because Phillips claimed it was): "Rocket 88," released in April 1951, a song hailing the greatness of the titular Oldsmobile coupe. It was so-called race music that Phillips was most known for in the early fifties, however. Most of the artists who recorded there at the time were blues and

R&B singers, such as B. B. King and Howlin' Wolf, for record labels like Chicago-based Chess and Los Angeles–based RPM.

Phillips founded his own label, Sun Records, in early 1952, after a record he'd made for the duo of Jackie Boy and Little Walter—"Blues in My Condition," with the B-side "Sellin' My Whiskey"—was rejected by Chess. The first Sun Records release, in March of that year, was "Driving Slow" by Johnny London, and the label's first legitimate hit was "Bear Cat," recorded by WDIA disc jockey and R&B singer Rufus Thomas, a sharecropper's son from Mississippi who had made his name performing at the Elks Club on Beale Street. "Bear Cat" was an "answer record" to "Hound Dog," a hit for blues artist Big Mama Thornton and later a chart-topper for Elvis. After the Memphis Recording Service began sharing its space with the offices of the Sun record label, it became known as Sun Studio.

"i sing all kinds"

Marion Keisker told Elvis biographer Peter Guralnick about the day in 1953 when she first met Elvis, recalling a shy, polite eighteen-year-old "cradling his battered, beat-up child's guitar" and approaching her with a plaintive neediness in his eyes. He had passed the Sun Studio storefront many times; finally, one day, he worked up the courage to walk in and inquire, in a hesitant, mumbling voice, how much it would cost to make a recording. Marion told him it would cost $3.98 plus tax. Elvis paid for it with money his boss had advanced him.

Marion and Elvis's conversation while waiting to set up the recording equipment has become the stuff of legend. Marion asked him, "What kind of a singer are you?" Elvis responded, "I sing all kinds." She asked him whom he sounded like. His response: "I don't sound like nobody."

The first song that Elvis recorded at Sun Studio was the 1948 pop ballad "My Happiness," by John and Sandra Steele. Keisker and Phillips (who was listening in the recording booth) heard something in Elvis's version of the song—and in the one he performed for the B-side, "That's When Your Heartaches Begin," a 1941 hit for the Ink Spots—that set him apart. There was a deep, yearning quality in his still-immature, trembling voice that moved Phillips to save the recording with the notation, "Good ballad singer. Hold." Elvis walked out of the studio that day with a two-sided acetate record, and perhaps a bit more confidence than he'd had when he came in. For months afterward, Elvis would stop by Sun Studio, usually engaging Keisker in conversation (Phillips was often busy making records) and asking if she knew of any local bands that needed a singer. Invariably the answer was no, but Keisker took a maternal shine to the earnest young man and became nearly as convinced as he was that his big break was soon to come.

singing for the lord

In 1954, while waiting for that big break, Elvis was also starting to discover the spirituality that would influence both his life and his music in significant ways. The Presleys had been churchgoing folk back in East Tupelo, members of the First Assembly of God Church, but it took them a while to find a Pentecostal house of worship in Memphis where they felt they belonged. During their first few years in Memphis, Elvis and his family attended services at nearby churches or missions, but only occasionally.

Once the family picked a church, they began to attend more regularly. The **(16) First Assembly of God Church** was located at 1084 McLemore Avenue in South Memphis. It had humble beginnings, with its congregation first gathering in a tent and then a small storefront on South Third Street, before finally moving to the church building. It was one of the most popular churches in Memphis, with a congregation of some two thousand who came to hear the fire-and-brimstone sermons of the charismatic pastor, James Hamill, as he railed against the evils of activities such as movies and dancing.

The church might have seemed an odd fit for Elvis, except for the fact that the congregation included the members of the Blackwood Brothers Quartet, his favorite gospel group. The quartet was formed in Choctaw County, Mississippi, in 1934 and originally consisted of brothers James, Doyle, and Roy, along with Roy's son R. W., although its membership changed over the years. The group shot to national fame after appearing on *Arthur Godfrey's Talent Scouts* in June 1954. (Tragically, only two weeks after that performance, members R. W. Blackwood and Bill Lyles perished in a plane crash. They were replaced by J. D. Sumner and R. W.'s brother, Cecil.)

The Blackwood Brothers were the first gospel group to sell over a million records, and, in 1954, the first signed to a major label (RCA, the same one that would sign Elvis shortly thereafter). They had joined the congregation in 1950, and when in town they sang with the church's hundred-voice choir, which was renowned throughout the South. They also performed at the popular all-night gospel sing-alongs at Ellis Auditorium; a member of Elvis's first band, guitarist Scotty Moore, recalled that R. W. Blackwood would sometimes let Elvis sneak in the back door to attend, because he could not afford a ticket.

It was also through his church that Elvis met his first serious girlfriend, Dixie Locke, a student at nearby South Side High. Dixie met Elvis at a Sunday morning Bible study class in early 1954, and they dated regularly for the next two years; Elvis took her to her South Side High senior prom in 1955. Dixie shared Elvis's love of gospel music and even attended the funeral of R. W. Blackwood and Bill Lyles with him.

Today, the church is no longer a Pentecostal house of worship; it houses the nondenominational Alpha Church Congregation. Memphis's modern diversity of religious faiths is another way in which the city reflects Elvis, who, though raised a strict Christian, became intensely interested in world religions. Memphis is located in the heart of the so-called Bible Belt, and today the city is home to dozens of megachurches. Protestant Christians make up a majority of the religious population, but the city also hosts vibrant communities of Jewish, Catholic, Hindu, Muslim, and Buddhist believers.

jamming with the wranglers

June 1954 was an emotional month for Elvis. His sadness over the tragedy that befell the Blackwoods was balanced by an exciting opportunity that came his way on Saturday, June 26. That day, Marion Keisker called him into the studio to record a song that Phillips had acquired in Nashville called "Without You." Elvis rushed over ("I was there before she put down the phone," he later said) and got to work. His rendition didn't wow Phillips, but Sam encouraged Elvis to keep on singing whatever came to him. And Elvis did, for nearly three hours, belting out spirituals, pop songs, and everything in between. The marathon session yielded no concrete hits, partly because Phillips at one point stopped recording and simply listened, but by the end of it, Phillips was sold on Elvis Presley as a diamond in the rough.

Phillips booked Elvis for another session, this time with two local musicians, Scotty Moore and Bill Black, who played lead guitar and bass, respectively, for a country-and-western band called the Starlite Wranglers. Bill was the older brother of Johnny Black, one of Elvis's childhood friends, and, like Elvis, had attended Humes High. Elvis, Scotty, and Bill attempted versions of "Harbor Lights" and "I Love You Because," neither of which impressed Phillips.

The song that made Phillips sit up and take notice was an up-tempo take on "That's All Right (Mama)," a longtime favorite of Elvis's, by Delta blues singer Arthur "Big Boy" Crudup, which came about when Elvis and his band kicked off an informal jam session during a break. Phillips knew immediately that he had found the sound he was looking for. Elvis sang the song with a confident exuberance, while Scotty and Bill contributed a stripped-down accompaniment with a lack of instrumental flourishes. The vocals had a raw, slightly immature edge that would mellow out over the years with nary a hint of the Tupelo drawl that was recognizable in Elvis's speaking voice. It was a sound that was somehow both unique and universal. Within a few days, Elvis, Scotty, and Bill had produced their first Sun record: "That's All Right" on the A-side, and their version of Bill Monroe's bluegrass hit

"Blue Moon of Kentucky" on the B-side. The foundation of a mutually beneficial, if relatively short-lived, business relationship was forged, and a new musical genre was born: rockabilly, a fusion of traditional country "hillbilly" music with a speeded-up style of rhythm and blues. Before long, rockabilly would evolve into rock 'n' roll.

airtime with daddy-o

Now that he had a recording by Elvis, Sam Phillips had to get someone to play it. This is where another Phillips, no relation to Sam, enters the story. "Daddy-O" Dewey Phillips was one of Memphis's most beloved and eccentric radio personalities, a pioneer both in his manic verbal style and in the eclectic playlists that he programmed for his audience, often exhorting them to go out and buy records or other products and "tell 'em Phillips sent you!" Some say it is Phillips rather than Northeastern disc jockey Alan Freed who should be credited as radio's "inventor of rock 'n' roll." Phillips's radio program, *Red Hot and Blue*, which he simulcast on local televisions years before Dick Clark started *American Bandstand,* was aimed at the underserved—at that point, largely undiscovered—market of teenage music lovers hungry for something different. Phillips even played records "in stereo" before stereo existed by playing two copies of the same record on different turntables.

Red Hot and Blue was a mainstay of WHBQ radio, which broadcast from the mezzanine of a downtown Memphis hotel, the **(17) Hotel Chisca**, at 272 South Main Street. Once the largest hotel in its district, the eight-story Chisca (its name seems to have been derived from "Chickasaw," the name of the tribe that once occupied the Memphis area) was built in 1913 and was more utilitarian and less luxurious than the Peabody. Many of the rooms were built without bathrooms because its builders figured the hotel would be catering to tradesmen, who were not known for bathing regularly. Over the years, the hotel has contained a barbershop, a beauty parlor, stores selling cigars and liquor, and the headquarters of the Yellow Cab Company. In 1949, WHBQ set up broadcast facilities at the hotel, and on the night of July 7, 1954, the hotel staked a claim in musical history as the site from which Elvis Presley's first record was broadcast.

Sam had played "That's All Right" for Dewey (with whom he had previously worked in radio) the day before; Dewey was somewhat perplexed by it and had to agree with what Sam had told him earlier: "It's not black, it's not white, it's not pop, it's not country." Dewey phoned Sam the next morning and told him he couldn't get the song out of his head and that he was going to play it that night. Sam called Elvis to let him know. At home, Elvis changed the radio station to WHBQ and told his parents to keep it there and listen later.

Dewey played "That's All Right" not once but seven times in a row that night; the phone calls that came in from listeners left little doubt that he could have played it a dozen more. The overwhelmingly positive response moved him to telephone the Presley home to ask if Elvis could come over to the studio for a live interview. But Elvis was not there.

Where was Elvis during this milestone broadcast? He was watching a movie at the **(18) Suzore No. 2** theater at 279 North Main Street, too nervous to listen to himself on the radio. Gladys and Vernon heeded Dewey's desperate request to "get that cotton-pickin' son of yours down to the station" and ran over to the theater, each going down an aisle to find him and send him over to the Chisca.

Elvis was afraid that he would freeze up while being interviewed, but Dewey had a clever, if not altogether honest, plan to pull off the interview without a hitch. He played a few records over the air and left the microphone on while engaging Elvis in casual conversation, under the pretext of preparing for the actual interview. "Mr. Phillips, I don't know nothing about being interviewed," Elvis said. "Just don't say nothing dirty" was Dewey's response. Dewey asked Elvis where he went to high school, and Elvis said, "Humes," which communicated to his audience that he was, in fact, white; many of those who heard the song thought it must have been performed by a black singer, especially knowing that Dewey played a lot of "colored music." After a few minutes of such chitchat, Dewey thanked Elvis for his time. Elvis, confused, asked, "Aren't you gonna interview me?" Dewey replied that he already had—whereupon, Dewey recalled, Elvis broke out in a cold sweat.

After WHBQ had gone through numerous ownership changes and relocated, the Chisca began the next phase of its existence, as headquarters for the Church of God in Christ. The Snowden family, which had owned the hotel, sold it to the church for $10 in 1971. The church stayed there throughout the 1990s, until the high costs of maintaining the old hotel became prohibitive, occasioning a move to the nearby Mason Temple. The Hotel Chisca today stands abandoned, though visitors to nearby Elvis Presley Plaza on Beale Street might still see the hotel's sign and radio antennas. WHBQ, now a sports station, broadcasts from the Memphis area on 560 AM, airing University of Mississippi basketball and football games and baseball games of the Memphis Redbirds, the triple-A minor league team of the St. Louis Cardinals in the Pacific Coast League. As for the Suzore No. 2, it was torn down in 1981, and a modern office tower now stands in its place.

rockin' the shell

The enthusiastic response to Elvis's Sun record inspired Sam Phillips to sign his new young star to a recording contract. The signing took place on July 26, 1954, at the Peabody Hotel; a copy of the signed document, which established for Elvis a 3 percent royalty on record sales, is now on display in the Peabody's history-rich memorabilia room. But it was not until a few nights later, on July 30, that Phillips and others got a glimpse of the phenomenon that Elvis Presley was soon to become. This was the night that Elvis, Scotty, and Bill performed as the opening act for yodeling country music star Slim Whitman in an outdoor concert at one of Memphis's biggest and most popular live entertainment venues, the Overton Park Shell, today called the **(19) Levitt Shell**.

Ads for the show started running a week before, one misspelling Elvis's name as "Ellis," and most focusing on Whitman, singer of the hit "Indian Love Call" and the acknowledged star of the show, especially among Memphis's large contingent of "hillbilly" music fans. Most of the crowd that hot, humid night was there to see Whitman; Elvis was nearly paralyzed with stage fright. After a pep talk from Sam Phillips, Elvis stepped onto the stage with Scotty and Bill. His knees were knocking as his fingers nervously fiddled with the microphone. As he launched into the opening of "That's All Right," Elvis was barely aware that the motions he was making were causing the crowd to erupt with wild abandon. He thought he was merely tapping his foot to the rhythm; in fact, he was on the balls of his feet and jiggling his entire lower body in a way that no one, including his bandmates, had ever seen from any performer before.

This momentous night was also Elvis Presley's first paid performance. Some refer to it as the first rock 'n' roll show. However, it was not the first time Elvis performed in Overton Park: he had sung there during his Humes High homeroom picnic in 1953.

Overton Park, a 342-acre expanse in midtown Memphis bordered by North Parkway, East Parkway, Poplar Avenue, and Kenilworth Street, is still a destination for music-loving Memphians. The park was designed by architect George Kessler and named for Memphis co-founder John Overton. Planning for it began in 1901; the park was completed in 1906. It was part of a comprehensive plan that eventually included the city's M. L. King Riverside Park and the Memphis Parkway System.

The park became the subject of a controversial, landmark U.S. Supreme Court decision in the 1970s. Highway planners issued a plan to demolish twenty-six acres of Overton Park to make way for a new interstate highway. Citizens organized and fought the plan in court. In the 1971 case *Citizens to Preserve Overton Park vs. Volpe*, the Supreme Court ruled in the group's favor.

The Overton Park Shell, built in 1936 and located near the southwest corner of the park, was one of twenty-seven such band shell–style outdoor theaters commissioned by the WPA during the New Deal era for cities including New York, Chicago, and St. Louis. The one in Memphis is among the few that remain.

The shell was used mostly for open-air opera and musical theater performances throughout the 1930s and 1940s, then for country-and-western and rock concerts during the 1950s. It has evaded being demolished three times. In the mid-1960s, the Memphis Arts Center took control of the shell and planned to raze it and replace it with a new structure. A petition to save the shell, circulated by the conductor of the Memphis Concert Orchestra, garnered six thousand signatures. In 1972, the shell was again targeted for demolition, this time to make room for a parking garage; again it was spared thanks to community outcry. Ten years later, a religious organization called the National Conference of Christians and Jews put forth a plan to restore the deteriorating structure. The group could not raise enough funds for the project, so the shell went on the chopping block once again and was saved this time by Memphis mayor Richard Hackett, who pledged to renovate the shell if a private-sector investor would fund an arts program to keep it alive. In 1986, a group of citizens formed an organization called Save Our Shell to provide entertainment programs there through 2006, all free to the public.

Large-scale renovations finally came to the shell in 2007–8, funded by New York philanthropists Mortimer and Mimi Levitt. The structure was renamed the Levitt Shell at Overton Park, and once again it offers free shows to the public.

Overton Park is also home to the Memphis Zoo, one of the largest in the country, as well as the Memphis College of Art, the Memphis Brooks Museum of Art, and a nine-hole golf course.

opening-day jitterbug

In September 1954, the **(20) Lamar Airways Shopping Center** opened in the triangular intersection bordered by Lamar Avenue, Airways Avenue, and Park Avenue, and Elvis and his two bandmates were signed up to perform at its grand-opening concert. Something of a local sensation since the Overton Park show, Elvis and his band had played a number of local venues in the ensuing months, and Elvis had fully incorporated into his act the gyrations that had driven the youngsters into a frenzy on that hot summer night at Overton Park.

The largest shopping center in the area at the time, Lamar Airways was anchored by a Katz's Drugstore and included Pic-Pac, Kroger, and Shainberg's stores as well as several shoe and clothing shops. The concert, on September 9, was organized by Elvis's Humes classmate Marty Lacker, who worked at Shainberg's, and another high school friend, George Klein, who was a disc jockey at a local radio station. The *Memphis Press-Scimitar* announced the event the day before, misspelling Elvis's last name as "Pressley" and touting the giant wooden "robot" Indian from which George would be broadcasting the show. (Lamar Avenue had once been a Choctaw Indian trail, and the opening of the shopping center—whose emblem was a giant paper-and-plastic Indian chief—was to be blessed by a Choctaw chief.)

The stage was set up on a flatbed truck in the huge parking lot behind Katz's. Elvis, dressed in pink and gray, put on what had become his usual show, shaking and swaying as he sang and played guitar. In the audience were two musicians who would go on to bigger things: Jon Evans, later a guitarist and keyboardist for the Box Tops (whose song "The Letter" was the first Memphis pop tune to become a number one hit), and Johnny Cash, who had recently been discharged from the air force and was attending the show with his first wife, Vivian.

Except for a smattering of naysayers—diehard hillbilly music fans who simply could not understand the appeal of this skinny, wiggling kid with the flashy clothes—the youthful crowd went crazy for the act. It was Elvis and the boys' biggest crowd since the Overton Park show; because they were the only act this time, they knew that this cheering throng was here to see them, not some bigger-name star coming on after them. The members of the band knew now, for sure, that they were onto something big.

The completion of interstate highways in the 1960s reduced the importance of Lamar Avenue as a major thoroughfare, and businesses along the avenue suffered accordingly. Today, none of the original stores remains in the complex, and both the Katz and Shainberg buildings have been taken over by chain stores.

night clubbing

Even Memphians who remember the Eagle's Nest nightclub find it difficult to recall exactly where it was located. It was on Lamar Avenue (Highway 78), near Winchester Boulevard, just outside the city limits, east of the Memphis airport; but the entire area has since been redeveloped, and no landmark marks its spot.

Back in the 1950s, however, everyone knew where the Eagle's Nest was—at least, everyone who enjoyed Memphis nightlife, and especially those who had fallen under the sway of the hot young local singing sensation Elvis Presley. By late July 1954, the local media had taken notice. From an article in the *Memphis Press-Scimitar*: "A 19 year-old Humes High graduate, he has just signed a recording contract with Sun Records Co. of Memphis, and already has a disk out that promises to be the biggest hit Sun has ever pressed." The article goes on to quote Marion Keisker, who points out Elvis's unprecedented crossover appeal: "The odd thing about it," she says, describing the success of "That's All Right" and "Blue Moon of Kentucky," "is that both sides seem to be equally popular on popular, folk, and race record programs. The boy has something that seems to appeal to everybody." Certainly, most members of Elvis's live audiences were white, but blacks liked his music, too, possibly because many of them recognized where it came from. Elvis's music was a phenomenon in an era when musical genres were designed to be as racially segregated as many other aspects of the culture.

The Eagle's Nest was part of the Clearpool entertainment complex built by the Garavellis, a family of Italian immigrants who had purchased much of the land in the area to use for farming. The club was owned by Joe and Doris Pieraccini, who also owned a swimming pool and roller-skating rink nearby on Lamar Avenue.

The club had a dance hall on the top floor of a two-story building, with an elevated dance floor on the same level as the stage. On the first floor was a twenty-four-hour restaurant along with dressing rooms for the swimming pool. The club, with a capacity of about 350, catered to a mostly white, middle-class country-and-western crowd from Memphis and nearby north Mississippi. Because Shelby County was "dry" outside the Memphis city limits, patrons would go "brown bagging" at the Eagle's Nest—buying booze at a liquor store in the city and bringing it along in a paper bag to either mix with or chase the Cokes and 7-Ups that were sold at the club.

Elvis, Scotty, and Bill—now known as Elvis and the Blue Moon Boys, with Scotty acting as manager—started playing at the Eagle's Nest in August 1954, at weekend shows hosted by local country-and-western DJ "Sleepy-Eyed" John Lepley. Sleepy-Eyed John was not a fan of the Sun sound, and when he played Elvis on his radio show, he opted for the more countrified "Blue Moon of Kentucky," the B-side, rather than the more popular and heavily promoted "That's All Right." However, Lepley was undoubtedly happy with the crowds that Elvis drew to his Eagle's Nest shows. Elvis and his band were usually a warm-up act for more traditional country acts; some patrons recall that the teenagers in the crowd would come in from the swimming pool to hear Elvis sing, then dive back in the pool before the main act came on.

Playing at the club became a regular gig for the band, and Elvis, Scotty, and Bill appeared there numerous times between August and November 1954 to audiences of mostly young people. One night in October, a man named Oscar Davis saw the show and was impressed. The next night, Elvis played a show at Ellis Auditorium headlined by country singer Eddy Arnold and the band he worked with, the Jordanaires. Davis was also in attendance. Backstage that night, Elvis was introduced to Davis and the Jordanaires. He told the band that he would love to work with them. As it turned out, he didn't have to wait long to fulfill that ambition.

♪♪♪♪♪

by the way

"rocket 88"

The original recording of "Rocket 88," which went to number one on the R&B charts, is credited to Jackie Brenston and the Delta Cats. Brenston, the vocalist on the song, was the saxophonist for the Kings of Rhythm, a band led by future R&B star Ike Turner. Turner and his band put the song together in a rehearsal session in a Clarksdale, Mississippi, hotel room, with Brenston on vocals, Willie Sims on drums, Raymond Hill on tenor sax, Willie Kizart on guitar, and Turner on piano.

B. B. King, who was making records with Phillips, had passed the word to Turner that Phillips's studio was looking for new talent for the Memphis market. Turner packed his bandmates, instruments, and equipment into a car to drive to Memphis. Legend has it that Kizart's amp fell off the top of the car, causing its speaker cone to break. (Turner has said that the amp was in the trunk of the car and that rain caused the damage.) Whatever actually happened, someone decided to stuff wadded-up newspapers inside the amp, causing the guitar to sound distorted, fuzzy, and saxophone-like.

Phillips liked the unconventional "fuzz guitar" and made it the centerpiece of the song's rhythm track. That, along with Brenston's over-the-top vocals, Hill's ear-splitting sax solos, and Sims's driving backbeat drum, gave the song a raw, energetic, textured sound that would become the trademark of Sam Phillips songs. "Rocket 88" was released by Chess Records and became a huge hit. Singer Bill Haley, best known for the early rock 'n' roll hit "Rock around the Clock," recorded the song in June 1951 and had himself a hit; some consider this version, rather than the Ike Turner/Jackie Brenston original, to be the first rock 'n' roll song recorded. In any case, whether one marks "Rocket 88" or Elvis's emergence as the birth of rock 'n' roll, its roots are indisputably in Memphis.

chapter 4

from stage to screen

By 1955, it was becoming clear to many people in Memphis that Elvis Presley was going places. He and the Blue Moon Boys followed up their debut record with several other hit singles for Sun, including "Good Rockin' Tonight," "Baby, Let's Play House," and "You're a Heartbreaker." Their regular gigs at Memphis live-music venues such as the Eagle's Nest continued to draw enthusiastic young crowds.

Elvis, Scotty, and Bill had also signed a contract to be regular performers on the *Louisiana Hayride*, a live country-music radio show broadcast weekly from Shreveport, Louisiana. Although this commitment made it difficult for them to travel outside the South to perform and promote their music, the regular gig drew a loyal regional audience as well as listeners on 190 stations in the twenty-eight states that the *Hayride* broadcast reached.

The *Hayride* was the main competitor to Nashville's Grand Ole Opry, where Elvis and his band had played in October 1954. Their version of "Blue Moon of Kentucky" did not go over well with the Opry's more traditional country audience; the crowd's tepid reaction was a huge disappointment to Elvis, who had always dreamed of playing there. It was becoming more obvious that his music was something altogether different from country music or anything else out there.

After committing to a year with the *Hayride*, Elvis quit his job at Crown Electric to focus on his music career. With Elvis's increasing popularity and the more grueling travel schedule, Scotty Moore could no longer handle his managerial duties in addition to his performing ones. Elvis signed a deal with Bob Neal, who became Elvis's new manager. Neal was a disc jockey at Memphis's WMPS radio station and had been the booker of the Country Music Jamboree at the Overton Park Shell, where Elvis had opened for Slim Whitman. The deal went into effect on January 1, 1955.

There was another managerial presence in the picture, however: the man who had sent Oscar Davis as an advance talent scout to the Overton Park Shell in November 1954, and the one who had first brought Elvis aboard the *Louisiana Hayride*—a slick, ambitious operator who called himself the Colonel.

enter the colonel

The story of how Colonel Tom Parker came to manage the King of Rock 'n' Roll is a uniquely American tale of personal reinvention and unbridled ambition.

Although Elvis's life has been well documented, Colonel Parker remains an enigma years after his death in 1997. Although he claimed to have been born in Huntington, West Virginia, he was not even a U.S. citizen, and his given name was not Thomas Andrew Parker. We now know that he was born Andreas Cornelis van Kuijk in Breda, the Netherlands, on June 26, 1909. As a child, he worked as a carnival barker, honing many of the skills that would serve him well in the entertainment business.

At fifteen, he moved to the port city of Rotterdam, where he found employment as a galley hand on a sailing vessel. A few years later, determined to make his fortune in America, he jumped ship while the vessel was docked in the United States in order to illegally emigrate. He never said good-bye to his family, and some biographers have suggested that the man later known as Tom Parker was fleeing murder charges in his native Holland.

With only enough money to sustain him for a little while, the young Dutchman joined the U.S. Army, taking the name "Tom Parker" from the officer who interviewed him. He served in Hawaii and Florida; eventually, during his second tour of duty, he went AWOL. Charged as a deserter, Parker was sentenced to solitary confinement by the army and then spent some time in the psychiatric ward at Walter Reed Army Hospital, after which he was discharged from the service. Parker's rank of "colonel," incidentally, did not come from his military service. It was an honorary title—colonel in the Louisiana State Militia—that he received from Louisiana governor Jimmie Davis in 1948 in return for helping with Davis's election campaign.

By the 1930s, Parker was in the carnival and food concessions business, where he began cultivating contacts. He married Marie Francis Mott, and the couple struggled to eke out a living during the Depression, moving from city to city to find work. Parker found his calling in 1938, becoming a promoter for country singer Gene Austin and discovering his talent at using his carny skills to pack in the crowds for the singer, whose career had been on a downswing. However, when Austin moved to Nashville to stake a claim in the booming music scene there, Parker did not join him, possibly worried about exposing his illegal immigrant status. Instead, he took a job as a field agent with the Humane Society in Hillsborough County, Florida. His fund-raising trips brought him to Tennessee, where he persuaded musical stars of the day to perform at the Humane Society's charitable events. Among these luminaries was Eddy Arnold, the country-and-western singer who recorded the hits "Make the World Go Away" and "Cattle Call." The cagey and ambitious Parker saw an opportunity to get back into the music promotion business as well as to get a foot in the door for the career he sought, as a manager of talent.

By 1945, Parker was Arnold's full-time manager, securing the singer many hit songs and raising his profile with TV appearances and live tours. For his services, Parker received 25 percent of Arnold's earnings, an astonishingly high rate. Parker's management of Arnold ended in 1953, when Arnold got upset about the amount of effort his manager was devoting to another client, Canadian-born country singer Hank Snow, perhaps best known today for his song "I've Been Everywhere."

Parker and Snow were a good combination, and they formed a promotional company, Hank Snow Enterprises and Jamboree Attractions—the promoters of the *Louisiana Hayride*, whose mission was finding and promoting young, up-and-coming country singers. In Elvis Presley, Parker saw a potential gold mine. His first step in securing a working relationship with the young star was booking him as an opening act on the Hank Snow tour, which exposed Elvis to a wide audience. Neal was Elvis's manager, but both he and Phillips acknowledged that Parker's connections could benefit Elvis's career and hence all their bottom lines. Parker's mission from the start, so it seemed, was to take over Elvis's full-time management and get him signed to a big record label.

On February 6, 1955, after Elvis's first Ellis Auditorium show, Parker, Elvis, Bob Neal, and Sam Phillips met at a restaurant across the street from the auditorium. The gist of the meeting was that Elvis was a major-league talent on a minor-league record label; Parker had connections with larger record labels, such as RCA, through his association with Eddy Arnold and believed RCA might be interested in buying Elvis's contract from Sun. Phillips, who took an instant dislike to the pugnacious, cigar-chomping Parker, was not interested in selling. After some contentious discussions, however, Phillips, Neal, and Elvis agreed to bring the Colonel on board as a "special advisor," as it was becoming clearer that Parker had resources and entertainment industry connections that Neal did not.

the colonel's coup

While Elvis was touring through the South in 1955, his family moved again, to a two-bedroom brick bungalow at

(21) 2414 Lamar Avenue, at the time a busy, bustling street. Despite their son's continuing success, the Presleys still did not have a telephone of their own, so they had to go next door to make phone calls. In the fall of that year they moved once more, into a rented home nearby off the main drag, at **(22) 1414 Getwell Road**, today the location of a strip of shops.

Elvis's association with Sam Phillips and Sun Records began drawing to a close in the fall of 1955. In between the grueling schedule of travel across the region—gigs in Arkansas, Louisiana, Texas, and New Mexico and throughout Tennessee—Elvis, Scotty, and Bill found time to record another bona fide hit, "Mystery Train," a song produced by Sam Phillips for Little Junior Parker back in 1953. The other side of this single was "I Forgot to Remember to Forget," an original composition written for Elvis by Stan Kessler. This record, released in August, was the last Sun single by Elvis Presley.

Supposedly, the moment that Parker fully realized Elvis's unprecedented star potential, the moment he knew he'd have to get his hooks deeper into his young protégé, was on May 13 at a show at the Gator Bowl in Jacksonville, Florida. At the conclusion of his set, Elvis playfully announced to the crowd of fourteen thousand, "Girls, I'll see you backstage." The response was pandemonium, with both male and female fans storming the backstage area and pursuing Elvis into the dressing room, whereupon they began tearing off his clothes and shoes. Elvis remembered that night as one of the scariest in his life. Colonel Parker, however, saw dollar signs in the wild eyes of the rioting teens.

The Colonel had been negotiating for months with other record labels, primarily RCA, to purchase Elvis's contract from Sun Records. At the same time, he had been slowly increasing his involvement in managerial and promotional duties for Elvis, gradually edging Neal out of the picture. In May, Parker booked Elvis and his band on the popular TV show *Arthur Godfrey's Talent Scouts* in exchange for control over any future bookings that might arise from that appearance.

Sam Phillips's signing of Elvis had brought fame as well as other stars to his record label and in effect made the city of Memphis the promised land for hordes of young musicians with stars in their eyes. Like Elvis, Sun pioneers such as Jerry Lee Lewis, Carl Perkins, Roy Orbison, and Johnny Cash bridged the gap between country and pop music and laid the foundation for a new musical genre. In addition to Elvis's early hits, Sun released Lewis's "Great Balls of Fire" and "Whole Lotta Shakin' Goin' On"; Perkins's "Blue Suede Shoes" (later covered by Elvis); Cash's "I Walk the Line" and "Folsom Prison Blues"; and Orbison's "Ooby Dooby."

But despite Sun's success with this stable of stars, Phillips was heavily in debt and unable to handle the financial requirements of Elvis's growing stardom. He was willing to sell Elvis's contract but, much to the Colonel's chagrin, was also well aware what that contract was worth. Phillips and Neal fielded calls from MGM, Columbia, Decca, Capitol, Mercury, Atlantic, and Chess—all the major labels of the day—but none made an offer that Phillips would accept. Ultimately, he asked for $35,000, a huge sum for an artist who was at that point still only a regional phenomenon. Even RCA, the recording industry giant that had been the most aggressive about seeking to sign Elvis, balked, saying that $25,000 was as high as it would go.

Parker and his assistant Tom Diskin met with Bob Neal and Sam Phillips on October 28 at the offices of WHER, a Memphis-based radio station with an all-female stable of on-air talent whose offices were located in one of the first Holiday Inns. (Phillips was an investor in the studio with his friend, Holiday Inn founder Charles Kemmons Wilson.) It was a tense meeting—Phillips was upset that the Colonel had been spreading rumors to his distributors that Sun was selling Elvis's contract, and Parker and Diskin thought Phillips's demands were unreasonable—but by the end, a deal had been made that involved a gamble on the part of the Colonel. He would front Phillips $5,000 by mid-November and then convince RCA to pony up the whole $35,000. After weeks of wheeling and dealing, cajoling, and playing all the angles, Parker got RCA to agree to the terms on November 15. When it was clear that the deal was actually happening—part of him was convinced it would fall through—Phillips felt a tinge of regret.

However, he quickly realized that the money he'd receive from the sale of the contract would make it much easier to launch some of the new artists he was working with and invest in other endeavors outside the record business. In later years, he said that the sale was the best move he ever made.

Career-wise, this was also the turning point for both Elvis and Parker, who would become Elvis's full-time manager under the new deal. Elvis, who was close to Neal and his family, regretted that Neal was essentially left out of the new arrangement, and Gladys made it clear to her ambitious son that she did not trust the Colonel. However, Elvis believed that hitching his wagon to the RCA juggernaut was the right move. The signing—attended by a gaggle of interested parties, including Parker, Snow, Diskin, and RCA head of specialty singles Steve Sholes—occurred on November 21 at Sun Studio.

sun rise, sun set

Sun continued to thrive for a time. Its success, and the increasing size of the groups recording at the studio, convinced Phillips in 1958 that he needed larger quarters. He bought a building at 639 Madison Avenue that had housed a Midas muffler shop and a bakery, and gutted its interior to set up two recording studios on the first floor; offices for A&R, promotions, and tape storage on the second; and the accounting and publishing departments on the third. Phillips's own spacious office, befitting his new level of success, was on the third floor and boasted a wet bar and jukebox. As the new decade dawned, Sam Phillips, the poor kid from Florence, Alabama, was a music mogul in the country's most dynamic music city.

The new studio officially launched in 1960, and Phillips soon branched out further by opening another recording studio in Nashville in 1961. Unfortunately for Phillips and Sun, the style of music for which the label had become renowned—underproduced and raw, with just a few instruments and one vocalist—was by then going out of vogue. At the same time, the music business was moving in the direction of the LP album over the 45-RPM single. Phillips never believed much in the LP; he said he had no interest in releasing a few hits amid a bunch of filler.

Phillips responded to the changing times by making records with a more conventional pop sound, but this move only made Sun records indistinguishable in style from their many competitors. Moreover, the "Memphis Sound" that Sun had pioneered had become co-opted by other labels, such as Stax, Hi, and Goldwax. The last Sun record, by a forgotten group called Load of Mischief, was released in January 1968.

For twenty-five years, the original Sun Studio building housed barbershops and other businesses. It was empty in 1985, however, when former Sun superstars Perkins, Orbison, Cash, and Lewis came there to record the classic album *Class of '55*. This reunion inspired Phillips to come out of semiretirement and restore the original site as both a working recording studio and a tourist destination, and it has served in those capacities ever since. Among the big-name rock and pop stars who have recorded there since are Ringo Starr, Tom Petty, John Fogerty, Bonnie Raitt, the Indigo Girls, Def Leppard, and U2.

Today, visitors to Memphis can explore Sun Studio and soak up the site's musical history. A ticket buys a guided tour that includes two floors. The second floor was used as a boardinghouse for Perkins, Orbison, and other artists who came to Sun to record. It has been refurbished as a museum of Sun artifacts, including the original "Memphis Recording Service" neon sign; Sam Phillips's recording equipment; record jackets, posters, and advertisements featuring numerous Sun artists; and some Elvis memorabilia on loan from the family archives in Graceland.

The tour includes the audio of the original "Rocket 88" and "Bear Cat," and the very first broadcast by Dewey Phillips of "That's All Right." It also includes film footage of Elvis's appearance on the Arthur Godfrey show, the performance that inspired future television shows, notably Ed Sullivan's, to film him only from the waist up to spare America his "obscene" hip gyrations. Downstairs is the original recording studio, which visitors enter in much the same manner Elvis did, by first stepping into the outer office, where Marion Keisker's desk and other period details have been meticulously restored, and walking into the studio. Because it is once again a working studio, there is a stage set up with a drum set and microphones, and Phillips's original recording booth overlooks the stage. Along one wall are guitars signed by artists who have recorded there, including Roy Orbison and Gene Simmons of Kiss.

Perhaps the biggest treat for Elvis fans is the original microphone he used to sing "That's All Right," which patrons are encouraged to touch and pose with. Vintage photos line the walls, along with a huge reproduction of the classic image of the "Million Dollar Quartet" of Sun artists—Elvis, Jerry Lee Lewis, Johnny Cash, and Carl Perkins—who got together on December 4, 1956, to jam, a historic session that became the basis for a popular Broadway musical, also called *Million Dollar Quartet*. The spot on the floor where Elvis stood to record his first single is marked with an X; Bob Dylan once visited the studio and kissed the X.

a new place to dwell

The first Elvis Presley single with RCA was "Heartbreak Hotel," a haunting tune cowritten by Mae Boren Axton, the "Queen Mother of Nashville," who was working with the Colonel as Hank Snow's publicist, and a Jacksonville musician and disc jockey named Tommy Durden. Axton and Durden had both read a story in the *Miami Herald* about a man who had killed himself and left a short suicide note with the grim message "I walk a lonely street." Axton thought that when someone ended his life, he left behind broken hearts, and thus the imagery of a heartbreak hotel at the end of that lonely street made for some powerful song lyrics. Supposedly the song was written in a half hour sometime in 1955. It was a while before Elvis heard it, but when Neal played him the demo, recorded by songwriter Glenn Reeves, Elvis loved it and agreed with Axton that it could be his next hit single.

The song was a risk commercially: RCA had invested an unprecedented sum in Elvis, and the brooding melody of "Heartbreak Hotel" was a departure from the up-tempo, rockabilly-style Sun singles that Elvis's audience knew and loved. But Sholes, who had become Elvis's producer at RCA, trusted the singer's instincts. Backing up Elvis on the recording were Scotty Moore and Bill Black, drummer D. J. Fontana, and two RCA performers from Nashville who were stars in their own right: Chet Atkins on guitar and Floyd Cramer on piano. Sholes created the song's famous echo effect by recording in a hallway in the studio. The resulting record sold 300,000 copies in its first three weeks of release.

Elvis's contract with RCA granted him a 5 percent royalty (up from the 3 percent he had earned at Sun), and the royalties from "Heartbreak Hotel" provided the windfall he needed to purchase a home for himself and his parents. On March 3, 1956, Elvis wrote a check for $500 as a down payment on a $29,000 suburban home at **(23) 1034 Audubon Drive**, east of downtown Memphis, near Audubon Park. Gladys, Vernon, and Elvis's grandmother Minnie Mae moved into the seven-room ranch-style brick house at the end of the month, just before Elvis went on tour in support of his first LP, titled simply *Elvis Presley*, on the RCA Victor label.

The album included songs recorded at RCA's studios in Nashville and New York City, as well as some previously unreleased material recorded at Sun. (The rights to Elvis's Sun recordings had transferred to RCA with the sale of the contract.) It also included Elvis's version of the Carl Perkins hit "Blue Suede Shoes," which, due to an agreement with Sam Phillips, was not released as a single for eight months. Perkins's version, released on the Sun label, was vying with "Heartbreak Hotel" for the number one spot on the Billboard singles chart. Both Elvis songs featured the Jordanaires as backup vocalists, thus fulfilling a wish that Elvis had expressed when he met them backstage at Ellis Auditorium the previous year.

Elvis planned to settle in at the Audubon Drive home for the long haul, ordering expansions, additions, and redecorating touches that would make it his own. He built a swimming pool with a tiled mosaic image of a fish at the bottom, planted trees in the backyard, added new light and plumbing fixtures and wall coverings, and converted the garage into a pool house. He installed a slate countertop and a large theatrical mirror in the bathroom and had the halls wallpapered with a musical-note and piano-key motif. And then there were the lamps: Elvis at one point bought so many decorative lamps that Gladys didn't know where to put them all. Many of the touches were in keeping with the then-popular "space age" style, which is now considered kitschy.

The family ended up living in the home for barely over a year, and it then passed through the hands of several owners. In 1998, a married pair of writers and Elvis historians, Mike Freeman and Cindy Hazen, authors of *Elvis Memphis-Style* and *The Best of Elvis*, purchased the house and set about restoring much of its Elvis-era décor.

Considering Colonel Parker's original plan for disposing of the Audubon Drive house, historians are fortunate that it's still around at all. After Elvis closed the deal on his next and final Memphis home, Graceland, Parker tentatively agreed to sell the Audubon Drive house to a bubblegum company that wanted to raze it and then package tiny wooden pieces of it inside bubblegum packs, like baseball cards. However, Elvis had an exclusive contract with a rival bubblegum company, so the deal fell through.

"Heartbreak Hotel" became RCA's first million-seller, which must have made Sholes feel better about his deal with the Colonel and the gamble his company had taken on Elvis. However, Elvis's skyrocketing career was not without controversy. When his music went national, much of the media and the public reacted with outrage, blaming rock 'n' roll and its most famous practitioner—with his suggestive lyrics, long hair (for the time), flashy outfits, and pelvic-thrusting stage moves—for juvenile delinquency, race mixing, and basically what they saw as the entire breakdown of society and conventional morality.

To many today, having experienced some of the extremes of such twentieth-century genres as punk, heavy metal, rap, and hip-hop, Elvis's act might seem downright wholesome in comparison. For those who didn't grow up in the fifties, it's difficult to understand what all the fuss was about. Elvis himself did not fully understand the level of vitriol that certain segments of America were expressing toward him and found the criticisms unfair and unwarranted. He defended himself in numerous media interviews, telling reporters, "I'm not trying to be sexy," and "It's just my way of expressing how I feel when I move around." At times, he would point out that the "colored" musicians he listened to growing up did some of the same types of things and it didn't cause an outcry. Of course, in those less enlightened times, that may have been precisely the wrong thing to say.

taking tinseltown

In the midst of the hullabaloo over his music, however, Elvis Presley was on the verge of conquering another part of the entertainment world. He traveled to the West Coast in March 1956 for a screen test with Hal Wallis, the veteran movie producer behind such films as *Casablanca, Sergeant York,* and *The Maltese Falcon.* Wallis had seen Elvis on TV and was impressed with his talent as well as his ability to draw a youthful audience. Some producers envisioned Elvis as a successor to James Dean, whose untimely death in 1955 had left a cinematic void.

Elvis's screen test went well. He was not interested in singing in his roles—he wanted to be a real actor, like Tony Curtis, Marlon Brando, and the other stars he enjoyed watching on the big screen—but the first part of the test required him to perform "Blue Suede Shoes" for the cameras. Afterward, he acted out two scenes from *The Rainmaker,* a film that Wallis was shooting. Elvis, who had absolutely no acting experience or formal training, memorized the entire script rather than just his own part, and did a reading that impressed Wallis enough to sign him (after some brutal negotiations with the Colonel) for a three-picture deal with Paramount Studios. As with the RCA contract, the young man's raw talent, earnestness, and undeniable magnetism, combined with Parker's negotiating tactics, convinced a major studio to make a significant financial investment. Like Sholes and his colleagues at RCA, Wallis and his backers were not disappointed.

Elvis's first film was *Love Me Tender*—actually made for Twentieth Century Fox because Wallis couldn't find a suitable Paramount role for Elvis—in which he starred with Richard Egan and Debra Paget. Elvis played Clint Reno, the younger brother of a Confederate soldier (Egan), who marries his brother's fiancée (Paget) after she believes the older brother has died in battle. Predictably, the producers added some songs to the story to play up Elvis's singing, and he performed the ballad "Love Me Tender" for the film. (The song's title became the movie's, replacing its original title, *The Reno Brothers*.) The film did very well at the box office, earning back its $1 million budget in three days, but reviewers were hard on Elvis the actor in his big-screen debut, as they would be, with few exceptions, throughout his film career.

The beginning of that career heralded the next phase of Elvis's life, when he began to spend less time in Memphis and more in Hollywood. At first he was uncomfortable amid the trappings and traditions of Tinseltown, but his come-hither good looks and country-boy humility eventually won him friends, including actor Nick Adams, who had starred with Dean in *Rebel without a Cause,* and actress Natalie Wood, whom he dated briefly despite being, nominally, still in a relationship with his latest girlfriend, June Juanico, back home in Memphis.

Elvis had met June, a former beauty queen, in 1955 at a concert in Biloxi, Mississippi. She was close to Elvis's mother (and has been described by some as the only girlfriend Gladys ever approved of), and the couple were together for several years despite the many strains on the relationship wrought by Elvis's absences.

boob tube blues

Between the movies, touring, and recording, Elvis's absences from Memphis were frequent. In April and May 1956, Elvis made his first appearance in Las Vegas, as an added attraction to another act. At the Sands, he watched a group called Freddy Bell and the Bell Boys perform Big Mama Thorton's blues hit, "Hound Dog." He loved their version so much that he decided to do his own. The song was written by Jerry Leiber and Mike Stoller, who would go on to become an influential rock 'n' roll songwriting duo, writing and producing hits for Elvis as well as the Drifters and the Coasters. Elvis performed the song for a nationwide audience on June 5, 1956, in his second appearance on *The Milton Berle Show*. Scotty Moore added an energetic guitar solo, and D. J. Fontana contributed drum rolls between verses. Elvis practically snarled the defiant lyrics as he gyrated through the performance. "Hound Dog" became a hit and served as the closer for many of Elvis's live shows, but the song, and Elvis's performance of it, became critics' Exhibit A in the case against rock 'n' roll in general—and Elvis in particular—as a corrupting influence on America's youth.

The song and the controversy it generated led to one of Elvis's lowest professional moments, as a guest on NBC's *Steve Allen Show* in July 1956. Allen, no fan of rock 'n' roll, insisted that Elvis modify his image for the TV appearance, making him don a black tuxedo and refrain from shaking his body while singing. The experience was topped off by the humiliation of Elvis's having to sing "Hound Dog" to an actual hound dog—a basset hound wearing a top hat and bow tie.

During the filming of *Love Me Tender*, Elvis got another opportunity for nationwide exposure when CBS's *Ed Sullivan Show* came calling. Sullivan, who hosted the most popular variety show on TV, had once stated to the media that Elvis would never be allowed on the show because of Sullivan's objections to the "immoral" nature of his performances. However, Sullivan relented after Elvis's appearance on Allen's program—his biggest competitor in prime time—trounced Sullivan's show in that night's ratings.

Sullivan was less inclined to censor Elvis than Allen was. On September 9, 1956, though, Sullivan was unavailable to host, so Elvis was introduced by a guest host, actor Charles Laughton. Elvis performed "Don't Be Cruel" and "Love Me Tender" and was spared the restrictions that he had encountered on Allen's show. However, when he launched into a second set with his version of Little Richard's "Ready Teddy" and started gyrating, the cameras pulled in so the TV audience saw him only from the waist up. The episode set a ratings record, with 60 million viewers—more than 82 percent of the national TV audience—tuning in. Sullivan himself welcomed Elvis to the show on two other occasions, on October 28 of the same year and on January 6 of the next. Eventually, however, the Colonel's increasing monetary demands for Elvis's TV appearances so annoyed Sullivan that he stopped inviting Elvis on the show.

Perhaps the Colonel thought he was past the point of needing Ed Sullivan to promote his protégé. After all, Elvis had moved on to being a movie star. He started on his three-picture deal with Wallis and Paramount in January 1957 with *Loving You*, directed by Hal Kantner, about a young hillbilly singer who overcomes obstacles to become a star. It was clearly intended to be somewhat autobiographical. This film, in which Elvis costarred with Dolores Hart, established the blueprint for most subsequent Elvis movies—light on story, heavy on musical numbers, and undemanding of serious acting chops from its leading man. The sound track generated another number one hit, "Teddy Bear."

Shortly after wrapping *Loving You*, Elvis ended his relationship with June Juanico and began dating Anita Wood, a nineteen-year-old aspiring actress and singer from Jackson, Tennessee, who was hosting a local Memphis TV program called *Top 10 Dance Party*. On their first date, they rode around Memphis in a black limo; Elvis, like a proud little boy, showed off the life-size cutout of himself that was stationed outside one of his favorite movie houses, the now closed Strand Theater, at 138 South Main Street, as a promotion for his new film. A few nights later, Elvis rented the entire theater to host a private showing of *Loving You* for his family and friends and invited Anita as his special guest. Memphis was justly proud of its young star, and the feeling was mutual for Elvis. He may have been a Hollywood actor, but he still called the city home, and in the 1950s, Memphis, with its theaters, music halls, skating rinks, and parks, was a great place for a young man to impress a girl on a first date.

On the heels of *Loving You*, Elvis began filming *Jailhouse Rock*, especially memorable for its famous, painstakingly choreographed prison dance sequence. The routine was partly built around Elvis's signature hip gyrations, which he admitted were not really dancing. A slightly risky picture, *Jailhouse Rock* deviated from the Elvis-film formula in its gritty look (it was filmed in black-and-white CinemaScope rather than color) and the hard-edged, unlikable character that Elvis played, guitar-playing con Vince Everett. Elvis recorded the sound track for *Jailhouse Rock* with the aid of his new favorite instrument, the Gibson J200 guitar.

guitar central

In the 1950s, the three-story building at 121 Union Avenue, on the block between Second Avenue and Main Street, played an important role in the development of rock 'n' roll, selling guitars and other musical instruments to the Memphis musicians who were its earliest pioneers. The **(24) O. K. Houck Piano Company** counted Elvis as one of its regular customers starting around 1955, selling him several guitars as well as a piano that is now in the Graceland collection.

The company was a longtime Memphis institution, starting out in 1883 as a music-publishing company, O. K. Houck & Co., located at 359 Main Street. John Cassell Houck, father of the company's founder, Oliver Kershner Houck, was the manager of a nearby business called French Piano Company, which may have led to O. K. Houck's branching out into that business shortly after the turn of the century. In 1903, the corporate name changed to O. K. Houck Piano Company, and the business began to sell and rent musical instruments and merchandise along with sheet music. The company grew swiftly in the early 1900s, opening stores in Little Rock, Shreveport, St. Louis, Nashville, and Chicago (at one point, the company's address was listed as 245 Wabash Avenue in Chicago), but most of these stores did not last through the Great Depression. The original Memphis store filed for bankruptcy in 1933 but managed to survive.

In the 1950s, Houck's was unique because it catered not only to classical musicians (with pianos, organs, and such) but also to aspiring rock 'n' rollers (with its wide selection of guitars). Much of the credit for this probably goes to Thomas S. "Sid" Lapworth, an aspiring jazz musician who began working as Houck's instrument manager in 1954. Sid and two members of the Houck family ran the shop. Scotty Moore bought his Gibson ES925 guitar from Houck's in 1953 and played it during the early Sun recording days and on tour with Elvis and Bill.

Over the years, Sid sold instruments to B. B. King, Johnny Cash, Conway Twitty, and many others. He sold Bill Black his own upright Kay bass guitar when he realized that the store didn't have one in stock at the time. (This famous instrument is now owned by Paul McCartney.)

Elvis had purchased several guitars at Houck's before he acquired his Gibson J200 acoustic guitar. He'd first bought a Martin 000-18 from Sid, a small guitar that suited his budget at the time. He traded this one in for a Martin D-18 model and then, in 1955, a D-28. In 1956, the Gibson guitar company approached Sid to see if he could convince Elvis to switch to a Gibson. This would have been a huge marketing coup. Sid suggested that the company just give Elvis a guitar, which it was willing to do, but Colonel Parker nixed the idea. He did not want Elvis beholden to any brand or to give Gibson free publicity.

Elvis (and Gibson) found a way around this restriction, however. Scotty Moore was good friends with Tiny Timbrell, a fellow musician who happened to be the Gibson company's West Coast representative. Tiny signed Scotty to an endorsement deal with Gibson, so the company sent the J200 to Scotty and invoiced it to him rather than to Elvis. Scotty then presented the guitar to Elvis as a gift. (Supposedly, to accede to the Colonel's wishes, Elvis ended up paying for the guitar in full.) It quickly became Elvis's favorite instrument. Originally developed for country singers in the 1930s, the Gibson had a look and sound that was ideal for early rock 'n' roll. In addition to *Jailhouse Rock,* Elvis played his Gibson in *G.I. Blues* and *King Creole,* as well as at numerous live concerts. Later personalized with Elvis's name on the fretboard, the guitar is now in the collection at Graceland.

At the time when Elvis bought his first Gibson, the company made all of its guitars in Michigan. Now it also makes them in Memphis at its factory and retail store, the **(25) Gibson Beale Street Showcase**, 145 Lt. George W. Lee Avenue, one block south of Beale Street and across from the FedEx Forum. The company, whose home office is now in Nashville, traces its origins to Kalamazoo, Michigan, where Orville Gibson began making mandolins in the late 1890s. He developed, and later patented, a style of mandolin that replaced the flat, solid-wood tops and bowl-shaped backs (which he believed made the instrument too fragile) with carved wood tops and backs and bent wood sides, and applied the same principles to guitars. Gibson invented the arch-top guitar, incorporating the same style of carved wood tops. By the 1930s, the company was also producing flat-top acoustic models as well as one of the first commercially available hollow-bodied electric guitars. It introduced its most famous model, the legendary and still-popular Les Paul, in the early 1950s.

After several ownership changes, production moved in 1974 from Kalamazoo to Nashville, and the company opened up a handful of other factories, including the huge plant in Memphis, which manufactures classics such as the B. B. King "Lucille" and the Chet Atkins "Country Gentleman," along with other historic reissues and custom models. The facility offers tours on which visitors can see the guitar-making craftspeople, called luthiers, performing the tasks involved in assembling Gibsons, from neck fitting and painting to buffing and tuning. In keeping with Memphis's continuing love affair with music, there's also a lounge where live musical acts perform.

Armed with his state-of-the-art signature instrument—not to mention a very successful start to a career on the silver screen—Elvis was beginning to realize that he had traveled a long way from his impoverished youth, with its dime-store guitars, odd jobs, and cramped apartments. His astounding success, which he had feared could be fleeting, looked as though it might be here to stay. The newly crowned King of Rock 'n' Roll felt the time had come to give his beloved family the palace they deserved.

Elvis with his parents, Vernon and Gladys.

Elvis with Colonel Tom Parker, on the set of *Love Me Tender*, Elvis's first movie.

Elvis was proud of Graceland, the Southern mansion that became his home in 1957.

chapter 5

the house that rock built

In early 1957, Elvis's fame was beginning to impinge on his family's privacy and, perhaps more important to Elvis, to annoy his neighbors. The crowds of fans and journalists that would congregate outside the house on Audubon Drive—according to Elvis's cousin Billy Smith, some fans were stealing laundry right from the clotheslines as souvenirs—precipitated his decision to move to a larger, more secluded, more secure property. Elvis, for whom price was no object at this point, gave his parents a very generous budget of $100,000 to find a suitable place.

They decided on **(26) Graceland** (3764 Elvis Presley Boulevard, formerly called South Bellevue Boulevard, and also known as Highway 51 South), a 13.8-acre estate dominated by a white-columned mansion located in the upscale Whitehaven neighborhood, nine miles from downtown Memphis and four miles north of the Mississippi border. Originally a farm community, Whitehaven was developed into a residential suburb in the 1950s. By 1960, its population had grown to nearly 14,000 residents. When the Presleys moved there, Whitehaven was, in fact, its own city; Memphis did not annex Whitehaven until 1970. Whitehaven's population at the time was nearly all white, another aspect that would change drastically after the 1960s.

The original five-hundred-acre Graceland property was named for Grace Toof, daughter of its owner, S. E. Toof, founder of a Memphis printing company. Grace had left the land to a niece and two nephews. The nephews sold their share to their sister, Ruth Moore, and her husband, Dr. Thomas Moore. The Moores sold much of the acreage for subdivision and development but maintained a piece of it to build a country home where Thomas could raise purebred Hereford cattle. Appropriately, the house had something of a musical pedigree: Ruth Moore's daughter, only fourteen at the time of the sale, would go on to a successful career as a harpist for the Memphis Symphony Orchestra.

The eighteen-room house, designed by architects Max Furbringer and Merrill Ehrman, was built in 1939. It was constructed in a Georgian colonial revival style, with a tan limestone facade, Corinthian columns around the entrance portico, and two stone lions guarding the front steps. Originally 10,266 square feet when Elvis bought it, the house expanded to 17,552 square feet during the two decades he lived there.

Elvis bought the house for $102,500, with $10,000 cash down. Much to the chagrin of Vernon, who managed his son's finances with a thrifty Depression-era mind-set, there was very little haggling. As soon as the deal was closed, Elvis was gung-ho to redecorate. On the recommendation of Sam Phillips, who had recently moved into a new, luxurious home in the Memphis suburbs, Elvis hired decorator George Golden. Golden was a former Lipton tea salesman who promoted his interior decorating business by cruising around town in a flatbed truck displaying miniature scale models of rooms in glass cases decked out with carpets, wallpaper, and an item that apparently caught Elvis's eye, a big chartreuse satin sofa.

Golden recalled competing with two female contractors (Memphis had only three professional decorators at the time) for the coveted gig of decorating Elvis's new home. When all three were invited over to the house to make their bids, Golden engaged Vernon in small talk while the ladies set their sights on Gladys, who was overwhelmed by their aggressive approach. "Those two gals were all over poor Gladys, waving sketches in her face and gabbing like you wouldn't believe," Golden said in an interview. "Finally, she had enough. She waved her hands in those women's faces and said, 'Get away and leave me alone! Mr. Golden's gonna do our work!' "

The renovations were to be completed during the spring, while Elvis was in California filming *Jailhouse Rock*, which meant that Golden would be dealing more with Gladys and Vernon than with Elvis. Vernon gave Golden free rein to do as he wished.

Elvis's primary concern was maintaining his family's privacy and peace of mind, and part of Golden's responsibility was to keep the renovations a secret from the newspapers. Thus, one of his first projects was building a limestone fence around the property to keep the curious at bay. The big wrought-iron gates, emblazoned with a musical motif, came later. Today the limestone wall has been covered with graffiti by visitors to Graceland. Another aspect of Golden's agreement with Elvis was that he would not photograph any of the work while it was being done, which is why there are very few photographs of Graceland from the early days.

Much of the ostentatious décor with which Graceland has become associated was not part of Golden's original plan but was added by Elvis later. Having grown up in poverty, Elvis developed an almost obsessive desire for flashy luxury; he wanted his house to rival those of other wealthy entertainers and he wanted to show it off. Golden's original designs were more classical, using a variety of styles to distinguish the various rooms, none too faddish or too modern. The dining room and living room still display these restrained but luxurious appointments, with Italian glass chandeliers, gold-on-white trim, and swagged draperies. Elvis did insist on some unconventional touches, however, such as pink appointments and red, flowered bedspreads in his bedroom, and a ten-foot-long soda fountain, originally intended for a drugstore.

Even in a grand Southern mansion, you couldn't take the country out of the Presleys. With more acres of land than they had ever hoped to own, the family acquired all kinds of animals. There were horses, and Vernon kept hogs, which he slaughtered for ham, bacon, and sausage throughout the winter. The pump house behind the mansion became Vernon's smokehouse, where he cured and stored meat.

Elvis also bought chickens, ducks, peacocks, a turkey, and even, at one point, donkeys, which he kept penned in the empty swimming pool while the wall around the grounds was being completed.

Elvis was only twenty-two when he bought Graceland. Almost immediately, his home—like his music and his clothing—became a showcase for his highly individualistic, increasingly flamboyant personal style. But more important, in the heady years of worldwide fame as well as the later years of substance abuse and marital woes, Graceland was his sanctuary, where he surrounded himself with familiar faces and could truly feel like the "King" that the media had dubbed him.

inside the estate

Added to the National Register of Historic Places in 1991 and declared a National Historic Landmark in 2006, Graceland is now the most visited private home in the United States, second only to the White House in Washington, D.C. Today, the estate stands out like the city of Oz amid the urban blandness of Whitehaven, a predominantly low-income, minority community, one of many Memphis precincts affected by the "white flight" of the 1960s and 1970s in the wake of integration.

Every Graceland tour begins across the street from the house at Graceland Plaza, a property filled with Elvis-themed museums, gift shops, and a ticket booth. A shuttle takes visitors to the front gates and the now-empty guard station where security guards (often members of Elvis's family or the Memphis Mafia) once checked in all visitors.

Upon entering the foyer, visitors immediately notice the ropes that close off the staircase leading to Elvis's bedroom, his private office, and the bathroom in which he died. The aura of secrecy about the upstairs was prevalent even when Elvis was alive: no matter how lively and crowded Graceland became, few guests were ever allowed in the family's private quarters. As the tour begins, visitors learn that the bathroom, which, like the rest of the second floor is open to family only and not part of the tour, is located directly above the foyer.

What is fascinating about touring Graceland is that so little has changed since Elvis's last days there in 1977. To the left of the staircase is the dining room, with a black marble floor, white carpeting, and George Golden's chandelier hanging over the large dining table where Elvis ate at all hours and played poker with his buddies.

Less of Golden's touch is evident in the living room, to the right of the foyer, which features a mirrored wall, a white leather couch, and gold, blue, and white trim. Dividing this room from the music room is an entryway flanked by two ornate stained-glass peacocks. The central attraction of the music room, the site of many a late-night musical jam, is a baby grand piano. The kitchen is also on the first floor.

All the fixtures and equipment from the 1970s renovation of Graceland remain on display. Elvis's fixation with monitoring his property is evident here: a bank of video monitors is poised above the breakfast bar to help him keep tabs on the estate via closed-circuit cameras. If anything seemed amiss, he called security on the red phone next to the monitors.

Past the kitchen is the Jungle Room, which was originally a screened-in patio. With its over-the-top tropical-themed décor, the Jungle Room was what today we might call a "man cave," a place where the head of the household could relax in privacy. One of the room's other highlights is a portable telephone from 1966, a device roughly the size of a suitcase. Tracks for Elvis's final two albums, *From Elvis Presley Boulevard, Memphis, Tennessee* and *Moody Blue*, were recorded in this room.

Other rooms where Elvis and his pals typically gathered were the billiards room and the TV room. The billiards room instigates sensory overload; every inch of the walls and ceiling is covered with matching pleated fabric, the same as what is covering the couches. (A total of four hundred yards of fabric was used.) Elvis's pool table in the center of the room was the site of many games between the King and his friends; there's still a tear in the felt tabletop where someone attempted a trick shot.

Although the television sets in Elvis's lounge-like TV room are dinky compared to today's flat screens, they were state-of-the-art at the time. Three TVs are mounted side by side so Elvis could watch all three major television networks at the same time from a black velvet sofa with gold cushions. The room was a home theater and entertainment center, with a pull-down movie screen and a jukebox. Elvis's own record collection is also kept here.

Elvis took up racquetball in 1974 and built an addition to the house to accommodate his new hobby: a huge, two-story recreational area with a racquetball court, workout space, Jacuzzi, and showers. Elvis's personal shower has a typical touch of extravagance: five gold showerheads. Today this building is a museum with a breathtaking floor-to-ceiling display of Elvis's gold and platinum records as well as other memorabilia. Also here, enshrined in glass cases, are several of the jumpsuits that Elvis wore onstage during his Las Vegas years.

planes, horses, and automobiles

The tranquility of the beautiful grounds, with their large expanses of manicured lawns and white picket fences, feels a million miles away from the bustle of downtown Memphis. One can easily understand why Elvis so loved his home and why it has become a shrine for the millions who loved Elvis.

Leaving the mansion, visitors come across the shed that served as Vernon's business office and catch a glimpse of the Graceland stables, where Elvis kept horses. His widow, Priscilla Presley, still keeps horses here, a few of which are said to be descendants of the horses that Elvis owned.

The final stop on the official tour is the meditation garden, which Elvis built in 1964 and where he, his mother and father, and his grandmother Minnie Mae Presley are buried. A sober stone marker commemorates each; a small memorial plaque honors Elvis's stillborn twin, Jesse Garon Presley.

Once back in Graceland Plaza, visitors can stroll down a tree-lined street, past a movie theater showing Elvis films, to the Graceland Automobile Museum at the south end. As Elvis's fame and fortune grew, he did not think twice about dropping huge sums on expensive cars for himself and gave dozens of them away as extravagant gifts. Several of these are represented among the thirty-three vehicles on display in the 13,000-square-foot building, including the pink Cadillac Elvis bought for his mother, as well as his own 1956 El Dorado convertible in bright purple; a white 1956 Continental Mark II; a 1975 Dino Ferrari 308 GT4 coupe; a red MG that Elvis drove in *Blue Hawaii*; and a 1973 Stutz Blackhawk, a favorite of Elvis's that he drove the day before he died. Elvis also loved motorcycles: the display includes several Harley and Honda bikes from the 1960s and 1970s. Other novelties include the go-carts and dune buggies that Elvis and his friends tooled around in at Graceland, as well as a John Deere tractor.

Parked near the Automobile Museum are Elvis's two private airplanes. The larger one, the *Lisa Marie*, which Elvis called his "flying Graceland," is a veritable museum of its own. Elvis bought the spacious Convair 880 from Delta Airlines in 1975. He paid $250,000 for the plane and an additional $600,000 to customize it, employing the same team that had recently customized the interior of Air Force One. The interior of the *Lisa Marie* has been largely preserved and includes a queen-size bed, gold bathroom fixtures, a teakwood conference table, four televisions with a videotaping system, and a sound system with fifty-two speakers. The smaller jet is the *Hound Dog II*, a Lockheed JetStar custom ten-seater.

Across the street from Graceland is the Heartbreak Hotel, a 128-room boutique hotel erected in 1996. It is an ideal home base for Memphis visitors whose trip revolves around Graceland. Each room features blond wood furnishings evocative of 1950s interiors and framed black-and-white Elvis photos. There are several special Elvis-themed suites, including the Hollywood Suite, with its art deco, old Hollywood style that commemorates the King's movie career; the Burning Love Suite, decked out for romance with red and pink furniture, drapes, rugs, and bedspreads; the Gold and Platinum Suite, featuring a giant round table that looks like a gold record as well as replica microphones; and the Graceland Suite, which reproduces rooms from the house, including the billiard room and the Jungle Room. Elvis would have appreciated the Jungle Room lounge in the lobby and the hotel's big heart-shaped swimming pool.

feeling a draft

Even as an international star, with records topping the charts and movies packing fans into the theaters, Elvis could not avoid the responsibility that faced all young, able-bodied American men in the 1950s: compulsory military service. He had registered with the Selective Service when he turned eighteen, and received a student deferment that kept him out of the Korean War; when his draft number came up in late 1957, he received another deferment in order to finish filming his third movie, and the one for which he would receive his best reviews, *King Creole*.

Adapted from the Harold Robbins novel *A Stone for Danny Fisher*, *King Creole* was directed by Michael Curtis and costarred Carolyn Jones (who would go on to play Morticia on the TV series *The Addams Family*) and veteran film actor Walter Matthau. Elvis's role as Danny Fisher was originally intended for James Dean; it was the closest Elvis would come to filling Dean's shoes. Jerry Leiber and Mike Stoller contributed songs to the film's sound track, including the title tune. Elvis loved working with the duo, but they eventually parted company with the singer because they were unwilling to accede to the Colonel's contractual demands.

Elvis's military deferment lasted until March 20, 1958. Although it was peacetime when he finally reported for service, Elvis was worried. Not only was he unsure if his stellar singing career would be around after a two-year stint in the military, but he was also concerned about his mother—how she would get by without him and whether her health would hold up in his absence. One might have expected the Colonel to pull out all the stops to make sure his star managed to avoid service, but Parker took a different tack. He knew that such a move would alienate many of Elvis's fans and chip away at his image as an all-American boy. The very vocal segment of the public that was still scandalized by Elvis, or jealous of him, or simply didn't get him, was waiting for just such an excuse to validate their feelings.

It wasn't as if the military would not have been amenable to some sort of deal. Realizing the enormous security problems involved in placing a world-famous entertainer in a regular army unit and the potential PR benefits of keeping Elvis visible, the Pentagon offered several special enlistment packages, including one in which Elvis would entertain the troops at bases around the world while staying in VIP quarters. Another offer would have made him a "special ambassador," traveling to recruiting centers to help Uncle Sam sign up new soldiers. Elvis and the Colonel would have none of it. If the King of Rock 'n' Roll was going to join the army, he would do it the right way—through combat training in the field with the rest of the grunts. Eventually, the brass relented: Elvis Presley would enter the U.S. Army as a private.

Parker was engaging in a cagey gamble. If he played his cards right and continued to release Elvis's music over those two years while keeping the star tantalizingly out of reach—with just the right amount of media coverage—he could keep Elvis's legions of fans wanting more, making the singer's return that much more significant and profitable.

Elvis had taken his preinduction physical in January 1957 at the Memphis induction center at **(27) Kennedy Veterans Hospital** at 3000 Getwell Road, today the Delta Medical Center. It was not supposed to be a media event, but word got out, and a gaggle of photographers and journalists were waiting to document the moment. On March 24, 1958, Elvis reported to Kennedy again to be examined and processed, along with a dozen other new recruits, and to say a public good-bye to his fans before getting on the olive-drab transport bus to attend basic training at Fort Hood in Killeen, Texas.

The chilly, drizzly weather and gray, foggy sky matched the mood of the day. Elvis arrived at the hospital with his parents—Gladys crying and Vernon displaying little emotion—and his girlfriend, Anita Wood. The Colonel was already there when they arrived. There was a swarm of media that day as well, taking pictures and asking questions. Elvis reminisced to reporters about his early days of poverty and expressed his love for his country. He then hugged his mother and father, said good-bye to Anita, and, in an attempt to lighten the mood, said, "Good-bye, you long black sonofabitch," to his parked limo as the bus pulled away.

good-bye, gladys

Elvis may have been leaving behind stardom and celebrity for basic training and K-rations, but he felt a true sense of pride in his accomplishments. He had given his beloved mother what he had promised her since the Lauderdale Courts: a big, fancy house where she could live out her days in comfort and never worry again about work or money. However, Gladys did not enjoy her dream home for very long.

Down at Fort Hood, despite his often-intense homesickness, Private Elvis Presley, serial number US53310761, was adjusting to basic training. He was assigned to the Second Armored Division's Hell on Wheels unit, once led by General George Patton. Elvis displayed an aptitude for marksmanship (earning several medals) and gradually began to feel, and be treated, like "just one of the guys." He made friends with another draftee from Memphis, Rex Mansfield, who would later become a member of Elvis's entourage. Anita came down at the invitation of Elvis's sergeant and stayed in a house just off the base. Elvis was even able to squeeze in a recording session in Nashville while on furlough in June 1958. The session yielded several hits, released while Elvis was in the service, including "I Need Your Love Tonight," "A Big Hunk o' Love," "(Now and Then There's) A Fool Such as I," and "I Got Stung."

When the Colonel found out that army regulations allowed a soldier to live off base if he had legal dependents, he coaxed Gladys and Vernon into leaving Graceland to stay in a trailer outside Fort Hood. Minnie Mae and Elvis's childhood friend Lamar Fike also took up residence near the base, as did Elvis's cousins Gene and Junior Smith.

Crisis soon struck, however. Gladys had complained for several weeks about feeling sick; on August 8, Elvis put her and Vernon on a train to Memphis so she could be treated by her own doctors. The next day, she was admitted to **(28) Memphis Methodist Hospital** (1265 Union Avenue, today Methodist University Hospital) and diagnosed with a life-threatening liver illness exacerbated by a congenitally weak heart. Elvis obtained an emergency leave—he considered going AWOL if it wasn't granted—and flew to be at his mother's side. Unfortunately, Gladys's condition was too advanced to be cured. Vernon sent his distraught son home to Graceland to get some sleep; Gladys was pronounced dead of heart failure in the early morning of August 14.

Upon learning of his mother's death, Elvis was inconsolable; he grieved fiercely for days. He wanted her funeral to be at Graceland, the house she loved; but because of the Colonel's concerns about security, the service was instead held at the **(29) Memphis Funeral Home**, at 5599 Poplar Avenue. The Memphis Funeral Home would also be the site of Dewey Phillips's funeral in 1968 and Elvis's own in 1977. The Blackwood Brothers, Elvis's favorite gospel group, performed at Gladys's funeral.

Years before her remains were moved to the grounds of Graceland in 1977, Gladys Presley was buried at **(30) Forest Hill Cemetery**, just down the road from Graceland, at 1661 Elvis Presley Boulevard. Today, visitors to the cemetery will find the gravesite of Bill Black, who died of brain cancer in 1965, and Elvis's uncle Vester, who passed away of heart failure in 1997. Also interred there are several prominent Tennessee political figures, as well as Holiday Inn founder and Sam Phillips confidant Charles Kemmons Wilson.

At the end of the funeral, as the body of Gladys was lowered into the grave, Elvis voiced his sense of desolation: "Oh, God, everything I have is gone. . . . I love you so much. You know how much I lived my whole life just for you." Although Elvis's life was not over, it had changed irrevocably. Despite his loving family, loyal friends, and scores of fans, Elvis felt alone when he left Memphis to finish his army stint. By the time he returned, he was a different man, a bit more worldly and a lot less innocent.

Elvis married Priscilla Beaulieu in 1967, almost eight years after he first met her in Germany.

chapter 6

homecoming king

On South Main Street in downtown Memphis sits Central Station, the grand railroad depot built in 1913 by architect Daniel Burnham. It was the last project for Burnham, who had gained fame for his designs at the World's Columbian Exposition in Chicago in 1893. Central Station once shared its duties with another hub, **(31) Union Station**, built in 1912. Located on Calhoun Street between Second Street and Rayburn Avenue (now called Third Street), the beaux-arts building was once the largest stone structure in the city of Memphis. (Today, a U.S. Postal Service mail-sorting facility, built in 1969, stands on the site.) Together, the two stations coordinated the schedules of more than fifty trains each day into and out of Memphis. But they never saw a crowd of well-wishers quite like the one that gathered on March 7, 1960, to welcome Sergeant Elvis Presley to his hometown.

Much had transpired both on the home front and overseas since Elvis had last been in Memphis, which was to attend his mother's funeral. After an emotionally taxing period of mourning, Elvis readjusted to army life surprisingly well. He made friends, was stationed overseas, enjoyed the nightlife of Paris and Munich, and received his sergeant's stripes. His family and friends were able to join him, living not far from the base where he was stationed in Friedberg, in what was then known as West Germany. Vernon met a woman, Dee Stanley, whom he married in July 1960. (It took Elvis a while to welcome her as his stepmother.) Elvis developed a serious interest in martial arts, training with Shotokan master Juergen Seydel, regarded as the founder of German karate.

In the United States, rock 'n' roll had outgrown Memphis and become a national phenomenon. Elvis's influence was evident in the new crop of teen idols that appeared on the scene, including Fabian, Frankie Avalon, and Paul Anka. All the while, the Colonel worked feverishly to keep Elvis's music in the national spotlight, releasing singles at well-planned intervals; for the most part, his strategy was successful. But to the legions of Elvis fans who continued to listen to his tunes and read about his army exploits in magazines, nothing could compare to the thrill of seeing the King return home.

Amid the media frenzy at Union Station on that snowy March morning, the Colonel was beaming with pride and publicly joshing with Elvis, but inwardly he may have been breathing a sigh of relief that a risky move had paid off: after years out of the national spotlight, Elvis had returned as nothing less than a national hero. Even Frank Sinatra, who once famously disdained Elvis's style of music as "sung, played and written . . . by cretinous goons," was converted, planning a celebrity-packed *Welcome Home Elvis* TV special on NBC. Airing on May 12, 1960, it was Elvis's first public appearance in two years. His performance on that show demonstrated a new maturity in his style, a more toned-down version of the frenetic physicality of his pre-army act, but it still elicited screams of appreciation from the studio audience. The special got monster ratings (a 67.7 percent audience share), and it made it clear to any doubters that Elvis did not get rusty while he was serving his country.

parker's pad

The Colonel made the arrangements for Elvis's homecoming from his own home base in Memphis: a suite at the **(32) Claridge Hotel**,

109 North Main Street, today known as the Claridge House. The corner of Main Street and Adams Avenue had been the site of another hotel, the Arlington, which opened in 1880. It was replaced in 1927 by the more modern Claridge, intended to serve as an alternative to the Peabody, six blocks away, which was often too crowded to serve the needs of all the well-heeled business travelers who frequented the city in its heyday as a hub of the cotton trade.

Like the Peabody and Memphis's other historic hotel, the Gayoso, the Claridge was considered an elegant home away from home for the moneyed class and a major hub of social and business activity. The Colonel was almost exclusively interested in the latter. The seventeen-floor hotel was one of the first in Memphis with air-conditioned rooms and was known for its opulent lobby, ballrooms, and rooftop garden. Its most famous feature was the Balinese Room, a center of Memphis social life for nearly four decades, hosting performances by everyone from the Tommy Dorsey Orchestra to Elvis. Memphis's first official Elvis Presley Day was declared on February 25, 1961, at a luncheon at the Claridge attended by Elvis, the mayor of Memphis, and the governor of Tennessee.

The Claridge fell victim to the same urban blight that claimed many other historic Memphis institutions in the 1960s. It closed in 1968 and remained vacant for fifteen years. Unlike the Peabody, which reopened bigger and better, or the Chisca, which still stands empty and abandoned, the Claridge was put to a new use. In 1984, after an extensive renovation by new owners (who acquired it in 1980), it reopened as the Claridge House Apartments. It was converted to condominiums in 2004.

In 1960, the hotel served as the Colonel's satellite office, and now that Elvis was back in town, it was time for the Colonel to get the King into the studio and in front of the movie cameras. However, recapturing the glory of the pre-army Elvis was difficult, due not only to the changing times but to the complications that Elvis brought with him from Germany. One was a propensity for prescription drugs, which Elvis had started taking to help him get over persistent bouts of insomnia; the other was the young girl he had fallen for over there, who not only complicated all the other relationships in his life but also threatened to put an end to the Colonel's carefully cultivated image of Elvis as a swinging single.

meeting miss beaulieu

Elvis had enjoyed a parade of female companions since he started his singing career, but only a handful had any staying power. His relationship with his high school girlfriend, Dixie Locke, ended shortly after his Sun Records career began. His next serious relationship, with June Juanico, was doomed because of the Colonel's influence on Elvis: Parker encouraged the singer to play the field, dating as many women as possible for publicity purposes. Anita Wood, who had maintained a steadfast long-distance relationship with Elvis while he was stationed in Germany, had moved into Graceland. Gladys, who was close to Anita, had often voiced her desire that Anita and Elvis marry; Anita hoped to fulfill that wish. Although Elvis cared deeply about Anita, though, his behavior while in the army indicated that he was not committed to a future with her.

After the death of his mother, Elvis sought out various ways to assuage his sorrow and loneliness—and many of those involved women. He enjoyed the company of Elisabeth Stefaniak, a bilingual nineteen-year-old German American who worked as his secretary, answering fan mail from overseas, as well as eighteen-year-old actress Vera Tschechowa, whom he squired to the Moulin Rouge nightclub in Munich. But none made as much of an impact on him as a doe-eyed fourteen-year-old named Priscilla Beaulieu.

Priscilla Ann Wagner was born on May 24, 1945, in Brooklyn, New York, to James Wagner, a U.S. Navy pilot, and Ann Rooney. Wagner was killed in a plane crash six months later; in 1948, Ann married Paul Beaulieu, a U.S. Air Force officer from Quebec, Canada. Priscilla was given Beaulieu's last name and was raised to believe he was her natural father. She had a typical military family childhood—moving from base to base in various cities and states, making it difficult to set down roots or maintain friendships. The family found some measure of stability when they moved to Austin, Texas, in 1956. But Paul Beaulieu was soon transferred to a base in Weisbaden, Germany, and once again the family had to pack up and move, this time to a country where Priscilla didn't speak a word of the language.

Priscilla's first meeting with Elvis was not a chance encounter. She often whiled away lonely afternoons in the Eagles Club, a hangout for American families of military personnel. There, while listening to the jukebox and writing letters to friends in Austin, she met a young officer named Currie Grant, a mutual acquaintance of her father and Elvis. Grant asked Priscilla if she'd like to be introduced to Elvis; after he reassured her parents that he would chaperone their daughter, Grant made good on his offer by bringing her to a party at Elvis's off-base residence in Bad Nauheim on September 13, 1959. The attraction between Elvis and Priscilla was instant and mutual.

What drew Elvis, one of the most famous young men in the world, who could—and, by some accounts, did—have any woman he wanted, to the shy young Priscilla? She resembled a young Debra Paget, the beautiful actress who starred with Elvis in *Love Me Tender*, for whom he nursed an unreciprocated crush for years. Emotionally, there was also a connection: Priscilla's innocent, guileless nature was vastly different from that of the worldly women Elvis had encountered in Hollywood and overseas, and she seemed to be able to see into his soul in a way that no one else could. When they began to spend time together, Elvis behaved like an awkward, lovesick boy in Priscilla's presence, a quality that endeared him to her more than his good looks or world-famous voice ever could. He wooed her by playing piano at the Eagles Club (but not by singing; Colonel Parker prohibited Elvis from singing in public while in the service, because it would have been tantamount to giving away a valuable commodity for free).

At first, Priscilla's father was not enamored of the idea of his daughter dating a soldier nearly ten years her senior, even one as rich and famous as Elvis. Paul Beaulieu kept a tight rein on the budding relationship, and nearly put a stop to it when Elvis brought Priscilla home past her curfew. Elvis persevered, however, and he and Priscilla became close. When Elvis returned to the States, Priscilla was half-convinced she'd never see him again. A March 1960 issue of *Life* magazine ran a photo of her waving good-bye, with the caption "The Girl He Left Behind."

lights, camera, back into action

Romantic complications aside, Elvis eagerly and energetically threw himself into the busy schedule of projects the Colonel had lined up. His first film after his return to civilian life, which reunited him with producer Hal Wallis, took advantage of his army stint. In *G.I. Blues*, released in 1960, Elvis starred as a singing army tank crewman who aspires to own a nightclub in the States and romances a cabaret singer played by Juliet Prowse. The director, Norman Taurog, shot some scenes in Germany while Elvis was still stationed there.

His first album project upon returning was the appropriately titled *Elvis Is Back!*, released in April 1960, which he started recording in March. The first Presley album released in stereo, it hit number two on the pop charts and featured the talents of a number of former Elvis collaborators: guitarist Scotty Moore, drummer D. J. Fontana, pianist Floyd Cramer, and the Jordanaires. The sessions generated three number one hits, "It's Now or Never," "Are You Lonesome Tonight?," and "Stuck on You." The songs demonstrate an evolution in Elvis's musical style, combining elements of the jazz, blues, and gospel music that he loved while growing up. "It's Now or Never" was actually a reworking of the nineteenth-century Italian song "O Solo Mio"; Elvis's operatic performance on that song was a revelation to many. (One of Elvis's favorite singers, Mario Lanza, had previously recorded the song.) Once again, Elvis proved groundless any fears that the Colonel or the RCA team may have harbored as to whether he still "had it." That same year, Elvis recorded the first of his two gospel albums, *His Hand in*

Mine. (The second, *How Great Thou Art*, recorded in 1967, won Elvis a Grammy for Best Sacred Performance.)

Elvis was uncharacteristically enthusiastic about the prospects for his next two movies, *Flaming Star* (released toward the end of 1960, shortly after *G.I. Blues*) and *Wild in the Country* (released in June 1961), in which he finally had the opportunity to do straight acting. Much to his disappointment, however, neither of these films was as successful as *G.I. Blues*, which, despite mostly harsh reviews, made $4.3 million at the box office and was the fourteenth-highest-grossing film of 1960. This was enough to convince Parker—who called the shots on the movie scripts—that kids didn't want to see Elvis in serious roles; they wanted to hear him sing. The critics be damned, the Colonel thought, if cheesy musical comedies brought in the bucks, then those would be the movies Elvis would make. Although Elvis trusted the Colonel in just about every move he made, and had become wealthy in doing so, the singer's distaste for his big-screen roles continued to grow; as a result, so did a rift between him and his manager.

rock 'n' roll boys club

Another development that gave the Colonel headaches was the growing entourage of friends, relatives, and other hangers-on that attached itself to Elvis upon his return to America, many of them drawing salaries as bodyguards, drivers, and the like at Elvis's insistence. Parker (and Vernon, who also had little use for most of them) considered the members of the Memphis Mafia to be opportunistic freeloaders who were draining Elvis's bank account. They included cousins Gene and Junior Smith; high school friends George Klein, Red West, Marty Lacker, and Lamar Fike; and buddies from the army, such as Charlie Hodge and Joe Esposito. Later, Elvis's stepbrothers David and Billy Stanley joined the group, as did his personal hairdresser and "spiritual advisor," Larry Geller. At one point, the crew even included a pet chimpanzee named Scatter. According to Lacker, the group's nickname came about in 1960, after a crowd in front of Las Vegas's Riviera Hotel saw Elvis and his entourage emerge from two black limousines wearing dark glasses and black mohair suits, and someone yelled, "Who are they, the Mafia?" The group came to be regarded by the tabloid media as Elvis's version of Frank Sinatra's Rat Pack.

For those who knew Elvis, the development of a cadre was no surprise. As his career took him away from Memphis for longer and longer stretches of time, Elvis felt more comfortable surrounded by familiar faces. But the guys ultimately wore out their welcome with Elvis's female companions, especially Priscilla, and their often juvenile antics on the sets of some of Elvis's movies were not always appreciated by Elvis's costars or the film crews.

They were the *Memphis* Mafia, however, and they had as much fun in their hometown as they did in Sin City. Even though Memphis was a city on the verge of hard times—the national civil rights movement that had begun in the mid-1950s was gathering steam and African Americans in the South were ever more inclined toward disobedience of the Jim Crow laws—it was still a relatively peaceful and lively playground for Elvis and the boys. One of their hangouts was the **(33) Arcade** restaurant, at 540 South Main Street, between G. E. Patterson Avenue and St. Paul Avenue. Founded in 1919 by Greek immigrant Speros Zepatos, the Arcade is the city's oldest café, operating continuously since 1919. Located in the heart of what is now called the South Main Arts District, the spot is a throwback to another time; a big neon sign out front, boomerang-patterned tabletops, and electric-blue vinyl booths contribute to the 1950s-diner ambiance. A plaque on the building's facade proclaims its designation on the National Register of Historic Places; a plaque inside identifies Elvis's favorite booth, still with its original cushions.

The original Arcade was a simple, one-story wood-frame building with a potbellied stove for cooking. That structure was torn down and replaced in 1925 with the current Greek revival–style building; owner Speros Zepatos's son Harry took over the business in the 1950s. Throughout the 1950s and 1960s, the corner on which the Arcade was located was the busiest in the city, and business boomed. Elvis was among the regulars before his career took off, sipping malts during his breaks as a driver for Crown Electric.

Somehow the restaurant survived Memphis's economic decline, and the third generation of the Zepatos family (Harry's son, also named Harry) now runs it. The Arcade is one of several historic sites in what is now called Memphis's South Main Arts District, which encompasses South Main Street between Webster Avenue and Linden Avenue plus Mulberry Street between G. E. Patterson and Vance Avenues. The entire district, which also includes the Lorraine Motel, the Chisca, and Central Station, is a designated historic landmark, and it is easy for a visitor to feel like she has stepped into an earlier era, especially while riding the vintage trolley cars operated by MATA (Memphis Area Transit Authority) that stop along South Main Street. As its name implies, the district is filled with art galleries and boutiques, and the area is one of the liveliest in the city.

In contrast to Beale Street, much of which has been rebuilt and glitzed up for tourists, the South Main Arts District retains its authenticity and is often used by filmmakers who shoot scenes in Memphis. A scene set on Beale Street in the Johnny Cash biopic *Walk the Line* was actually shot on South Main. The Arcade alone boasts quite a cinematic history, having appeared in a number of films, including Jim Jarmusch's critically acclaimed *Mystery Train* (the Arcade's exterior also appears on the movie poster), the Jerry Lee Lewis biopic *Great Balls of Fire*, and *The Client*, adopted from the novel by John Grisham, who set several of his legal thrillers in Memphis.

Although the Arcade still welcomes customers, the **(34) Rainbow Rollerdrome**, 2895 Lamar Avenue at Dunn Avenue, a popular skating rink that Elvis frequented as both a teen and an adult, has been consigned to memory. In the 1960s and 1970s, Elvis often rented the entire rink so he and his buddies could play their hard-knocks games of War. Invented by Elvis, the game involved two teams, each with the objective of knocking down as many members of the opposing team as possible. A dangerous pastime that resulted in frequent injuries, the game was indicative of Elvis's reckless lifestyle after his return from the army.

The Rollerdrome was part of the Rainbow Lake entertainment complex, which included a large swimming pool, picnic grounds, and the upscale Terrace Room restaurant. It first opened in 1936, chiefly as a swimming area. The owner of the fourteen-acre property, Leo Pieraccini, added the skating rink in 1942. Rainbow Lake was a popular hangout for Elvis and many other high school kids in the 1950s, but a series of mishaps—fires, robberies, fights (including one at a rock 'n' roll dance party cohosted by Dewey Phillips that resulted in the Terrace Room's losing its beer license), and a drowning in the pool—took its toll on the business. The complex was slated to become a private country club in 1958, complete with a luxury hotel, but those plans never materialized. Another plan in 1963 to tear down the buildings and replace them with a huge department store also fell through. The Memphis AFL-CIO took over the property in 1969 and built office and meeting space there, only to have a fire damage it in 1975. The most recent business to take up residence was a food-processing plant for the Pancho's Mexican restaurant chain. Now the star-crossed property is a desolate vacant lot.

Elvis and his friends often went to the **(35) Memphian Theater**, at 51 South Cooper Street. Elvis always loved movies, but by the 1960s, he was unable to see a film without being mobbed by fans and the media. He would often buy all the seats in the entire theater so that he, his crowd of friends, and whatever young lady he was dating at the time could watch flicks in privacy. The art moderne–style theater with a classic neon marquee was built in the late 1930s, with more than 850 seats and a big single screen. By 1969, however, it was vacant, and the Circuit Playhouse Company of live performers took over the facility. They renovated it, halving the number of seats, and began staging live shows there. Since 1986, it has been called Playhouse on the Square, and today it is a popular cultural venue, offering live performances in all genres—including dramas, comedies, musicals, and children's programs—and holding acting classes. The Memphian name lives on in the adjacent bar that serves drinks and snacks. The current owners have not forgotten the building's historic connection to Elvis; they offer tours during Memphis's annual Elvis Week.

bringing hawaii home

Elvis's next movie, *Blue Hawaii*, was filmed at the Coco Palms Resort on the island of Kauai in March 1961. It featured Elvis as a surfing tour guide, Joan Blackman as his girlfriend, and Angela Lansbury (who was only ten years older than he) as his mother. *Blue Hawaii* was a return to the familiar theme of exotic locales, beautiful girls, and musical numbers, though some of the songs in this movie were better than those in the previous few, especially "Can't Help Falling in Love," which Elvis sang at the close of nearly all his live shows in later years.

Hawaii was also the stage for Elvis's largest live performance after his return from the army. On March 25, 1961, he played the Bloch Arena at Pearl Harbor, a show dedicated to raising funds to create a memorial for the USS *Arizona*, one of the eight battleships sunk by the Japanese in the infamous 1941 attack. All ticket proceeds were donated to the memorial fund. The fund-raiser was another marketing coup for Colonel Parker, who believed that if Elvis's postarmy career was to have any staying power, Elvis had to not only satisfy his hordes of youthful fans but win over an older, more conservative audience as well. The Pearl Harbor show was a big step in this direction.

The show was indicative of Elvis's generous nature, which he demonstrated in ways large and small throughout his life, but especially in his postarmy career. After his return to civilian life, he began an annual tradition of donating large sums to local Memphis charities at Christmas. He also recorded public service announcements and appeared in ads for the March of Dimes in its fight to cure polio.

The success of *Blue Hawaii* led to two other Elvis movies in Hawaii, 1962's *Girls! Girls! Girls!* and 1965's *Paradise, Hawaiian Style.* Not only that, but Elvis was so enamored of Hawaii and its Polynesian décor that he was inspired to bring it back home with him; the Jungle

Room at Graceland is said to be a direct result of Elvis's Hawaiian experiences. But the furnishings came not from Honolulu but from a furniture store in downtown Memphis, the **(36) Jolly Royal Furniture Store** at 128 South Main Street at Gayoso Avenue. Built in 1947, the art deco building once housed a Black and White store, one of a chain of department stores for working-class shoppers with locations throughout the mid-South. The name referred to the black-and-white tiles on the floor of the shops but might as well have referred to the segregated facilities: in those days of Jim Crow laws, the chain boasted of its two separate luncheonettes, one for white and one for black customers, and even touted the fact that its white and black employees washed dishes in separate areas.

Two legends have taken hold as to how the Jolly Royal came to provide the furnishings for the Jungle Room. One is that Elvis drove past the store window and decided on a whim to purchase all the furniture on display that reminded him of Hawaii. The other is that Vernon first saw the window display and reported to Elvis that it was the ugliest furniture he'd ever seen. According to this version, Elvis subsequently bought all of it and designed a room around it just to annoy his father. Both stories may have some elements of truth.

a farewell and a reunion

In the late summer of 1962, the increasingly strained relationship between Elvis and Anita Wood reached its breaking point. Anita was living at Graceland but had become suspicious, with good reason, of Elvis's not very well-concealed relationship with Priscilla. After Elvis's return to the States, Elvis and Priscilla kept in touch through letters and phone calls; in June 1962, Priscilla made her first visit back to the States, meeting up with Elvis during his recording sessions for *Girls! Girls! Girls!* in Hollywood. The reunited couple spent an idyllic few weeks together. Priscilla stayed with Elvis at a house he rented in Palm Springs and joined him and the Memphis Mafia on a jaunt to Las Vegas. The last straw for Anita was a letter from Priscilla that she found in Elvis's room, which led her to confront Elvis about the nature of his relationship with the teen. Convinced that Elvis was not ready to commit to her, Anita left Graceland and moved back to her hometown of Jackson, Tennessee. Priscilla went to Memphis that Christmas, her first one at Graceland.

In 1963, Priscilla's parents assented to her requests to move back to the States permanently. With the expectation of her eventual marriage to Elvis, she settled into a separate house on the Graceland estate where Vernon lived with Dee. Priscilla moved into the main house with Elvis only after she and her parents had secured a promise from Elvis of an engagement when Priscilla was of legal age.

As part of her agreement with her parents to move to Memphis, Priscilla finished her senior year of high school at the Immaculate Conception Cathedral High School, at 1725 Central Avenue, a Catholic school for girls founded in 1921 by the Sisters of Mercy, next to the Cathedral of the Immaculate Conception, mother church of the Memphis diocese.

With Anita out of the picture, Priscilla believed the last obstacle to a committed relationship with Elvis had been removed. However, the King of Rock 'n' Roll, while deliriously happy to have her back at his side, was not quite finished playing the field.

the lure of vegas

No American city is more associated with Elvis than Memphis, but in 1963, Elvis began to stake his claim to one that would become a close second: Las Vegas, Nevada.

Hard as it may be to believe now, Elvis bombed in his first Las Vegas performance—in 1956, as the opening act (along with comedian Shecky Greene) for Freddy Martin and his orchestra at the New Frontier Hotel. Elvis was billed as "the Atomic Powered Singer"—a nod to the nearby nuclear test sites in the Nevada desert—but his energetic act, which customarily drove young audiences into an appreciative frenzy, fell flat with the older Vegas crowds, who were accustomed to more sedate lounge acts. After that humbling experience, Elvis was in no rush to perform in Las Vegas again. However, he did appreciate the city as a vacation spot.

His love affair with Vegas was solidified in 1963, when he filmed the movie *Viva Las Vegas*, released in May 1964. Another love affair also blossomed at that time, Elvis's relationship with his vivacious costar, the young actress Ann-Margret. To this day, few details are known about the nature of the relationship, except that Ann-Margret has referred to Elvis as a "soulmate" and that, unlike Anita, June, or Priscilla, she seemed to fit in very well with the Memphis Mafia.

Ann-Margret's presence did cause some problems. The Colonel worried that the actress was taking too much screen time away from Elvis and that director George Sidney was using the film as a vehicle to promote her as a star at Elvis's expense. And the ever-present gossip reporters had a field day with Elvis's obvious on-screen and off-screen chemistry with her, even at one point announcing, wrongly, that the two were engaged. Priscilla, who was supposed to be Elvis's steady girl-friend and was living, quietly and under the media radar, at Graceland, was hurt and angry. The relationship between Elvis and Ann-Margret cooled down shortly thereafter, but the two considered themselves life-long friends.

Viva Las Vegas did well at the box office (the rumors about an off-screen romance didn't hurt, and the musical numbers were above average; the title song also became a hit). Perhaps more important, the experience of making the film kindled a greater appreciation for the city in both Elvis and the Colonel. Elvis wouldn't perform there again for years, but the city became a second home.

meet the beatles

While Elvis was making movies and having fun in Las Vegas, events were brewing in Washington, D.C., in late 1963 and 1964 that would have a profound effect on the future of Memphis. The landmark Civil Rights Act, a bill championed by President John F. Kennedy before his assassination in November 1963, was signed into law by Kennedy's successor, Lyndon Johnson, in July 1964. The bill effectively put an end to segregation and instituted laws meant to end all discriminatory practices against minorities. However, the years immediately following passage of the law were fraught with tension. With many Southern whites resentful and fearful of an expanded role in society for blacks, and some black leaders advocating more civil disobedience because the law in their view did not go far enough, the stage was set for years of racial conflict. In a Southern city like Memphis, with a large black population, discord was inevitable.

The other major cultural development in 1964 was the new musical wave that began to sweep the country. The British Invasion began in earnest with the much-publicized arrival of the Beatles and kicked into high gear with their first performance on *The Ed Sullivan Show* on February 9 of that year—an epochal moment in rock 'n' roll history, on par with Elvis's debut on the program in 1956.

Elvis met the boys from Liverpool only once, on August 27, 1965, at a house on Perugia Way in Bel Air, one of several Hollywood-area homes that Elvis rented before he and Priscilla got married. The meeting was likely set up by the Colonel and the Beatles' manager, Brian Epstein; Parker played it like the media event that he knew it could be, leaking word of the supposedly private powwow to the press.

Contrary to still-persistent rumors that Elvis was jealous of the Beatles' success and felt threatened by it, everyone who recalls the meeting remembers a friendly, amiable atmosphere—after a fairly awkward start. Even though the Beatles were at the height of their popularity in 1965, they were in awe of meeting the American star who had inspired them—perhaps too much so. As John Lennon recalled:

> He sat—Paul [McCartney] and me on one side of him and Ringo [Starr] on the other. George [Harrison] sat cross-legged on the floor. A huge color television was on in the middle of the room with the sound off,

while a record player was playing the latest tunes. We could have just walked in on an average Elvis at-home evening. Elvis obviously liked to treat everybody the same. He finally broke the silence that had fallen over the room. "Look, guys," he said, "if you're just going to sit there and stare at me, I'm going to bed." He smiled, and we all laughed.

The ice broken, the world's most popular young musicians began talking and jamming. The boys traded road stories; Paul even gave Elvis some pointers on playing bass guitar. The two managers—Epstein and the Colonel—chatted separately in Elvis's game room while playing roulette.

One of the Beatles invited Elvis to visit them at the house they were renting over in Benedict Canyon; Elvis gave a noncommittal "maybe." He never made it out there. In his later years, however, Elvis included a few Beatles songs in his live-performance repertoire, notably "Hey Jude."

doctor feelgood

Although the Elvis-Beatles rock 'n' roll summit went well, it was obvious that the Beatles, and other British acts such as the Dave Clark Five, the Who, and the Rolling Stones, not to mention new American acts like the Doors and Jimi Hendrix, represented a new generation of rebellious, cool rock stars, with new, envelope-pushing styles of showmanship that made Elvis's once-controversial late-1950s act look tame and dated. Furthermore, no one in Elvis's circle could deny his increasingly troublesome dependence on pills. It had started while Elvis was in the army: the insomnia and nightmares that had plagued him for years got worse while he was overseas. Homesickness, anxiety over his career, and grief over his mother's death combined to interrupt Elvis's slumber to the point that he began taking medication to help him sleep. Later, to maintain the frenetic nocturnal lifestyle that he adopted after coming home, he started taking different pills to stay awake. When he first started gaining weight, he started taking amphetamines, which were much easier to acquire in the 1960s than today and were regularly prescribed as an appetite suppressant.

Over the years, Elvis became increasingly dependent on various pills, at times even risking legal trouble in order to get them. Several members of the Memphis Mafia stated that part of their job was to procure drugs for the singer, often on trips to Las Vegas, using their names rather than his to avoid any negative publicity. After several of these trips led to arrests, it was obvious that Elvis and the crew needed someone who could more easily, and legally, obtain medications.

In 1967, Elvis made the acquaintance of Dr. George Nichopoulos, nicknamed "Dr. Nick," a man who today is regarded with antipathy, if not outright contempt, by many Elvis fans. For a time, however, he was one of the most trusted members of the King's inner circle.

Nichopoulos was born in Pittsburgh, Pennsylvania, to Greek immigrants, graduated from Vanderbilt University School of Medicine in Nashville, and settled in Memphis. He worked at the Memphis Medical Group, where he and six other doctors specialized in internal medicine. At first he treated Elvis for saddle sores from horseback riding, but eventually he began prescribing pills for the singer's frequent bouts of insomnia. For a while, Dr. Nick maintained his practice at the Memphis Medical Group and treated Elvis only when the singer was in town. Eventually, however, Dr. Nick accompanied the entourage on tour, his medical bag at the ready. By 1970, Dr. Nick was an honorary member of the Memphis Mafia and Elvis's go-to guy for pills and prescriptions. Nichopoulos recalled that when he took on Elvis as a patient, the star was already taking an array of uppers and downers, including Tiunal, Desbutal, Escatrol, and Placidyl. "Elvis's problem was that he didn't see the wrong in it," Nichopoulos told a reporter. "He felt that by getting it from a doctor, he wasn't the common, everyday junkie getting something off the street. He was a person who thought that as far as medicines and drugs went, there was something for everything."

two weddings and a birth

For several years, Priscilla Beaulieu waited patiently for the promised engagement ring from Elvis, living secretly at Graceland and tolerating the star's long absences, dalliances with other women, and what even she recognized was a growing drug problem. Around Christmas of 1966, possibly prodded by Priscilla's father, Elvis finally proposed.

Elvis had been agonizing over the decision to propose for a while, and he had ordered a pair of wedding rings from a friend he had known since high school, Harry Levitch, owner of **(37) Harry Levitch Jewelers**, at 5100 Poplar Avenue. Elvis had begun patronizing the shop in the early 1960s, and Levitch had produced several significant items for Elvis, including another ring that some friends thought was an engagement ring for Priscilla but turned out to be a gift for his grandmother to replace one she had lost. Levitch also created the Star of David wristwatches that Elvis began giving away to friends in 1965 as symbols of universal brotherhood—one of the many outward expressions of Elvis's growing interest in religion, which had been stoked by Larry Geller, who was Jewish. When Elvis was finally ready to propose, Levitch sold him the engagement ring, which featured a three-and-a-half-carat diamond encircled by a row of smaller, detachable diamonds, as well as the wedding bands, which had been sitting in a safe at Levitch's jewelry store for months while Elvis worked up his courage to take this major step.

Harry Levitch remained friends with Elvis throughout his life. He died in 2003, and his family-owned store closed shortly thereafter. His son, Ronald Levitch, continues the family trade at Accent Jewelers, 5050 Poplar Avenue.

Elvis and Priscilla's small, secretive wedding was held on May 1, 1967, at the Aladdin Hotel in Las Vegas. The couple held a reception at Graceland on May 29 that included all the members of Elvis's widening circle of friends and handlers, some of whom were resentful about not being included in the real ceremony.

The newlyweds spent part of their honeymoon at the Circle G Ranch, a 163-acre property across the state line in Mississippi, which

Elvis had bought earlier that year. He and Priscilla both loved riding horses, and the ranch offered more space to roam than Graceland. They bought a home on Hillcrest Road in Beverly Hills, close to the movie sets of Hollywood where Elvis was spending more and more of his time. In fact, the only Presley singles released during the mid- to late 1960s were from movie sound tracks. He essentially stopped making albums and performing live. And while he expressed growing disdain for his movie roles, there was one very challenging and pressing role awaiting him—nine months to the day after his wedding to Priscilla.

Founded in 1912, **(38) Baptist Memorial Hospital**, 6019 Walnut Grove Road, was the site of several medical-industry firsts. At one point the largest privately owned hospital in the South, it was one of the first in the mid-South region with automatic elevators and air-conditioning and the first to offer physical therapy, as well as the first in the nation to install a computer for accounts billing. On February 1, 1968, it made history as the birthplace of Lisa Marie Presley, Elvis and Priscilla's only child. Today, the Baptist Memorial health care system includes fourteen affiliate hospitals throughout the mid-South.

comeback kid

The chaos and cultural upheavals that reached their peak in 1968—King's assassination, Democratic presidential candidate Robert Kennedy's murder in Los Angeles, and the hippie culture that glorified drugs and free love—had a profound impact on Elvis's career. Worse, events had made his beloved Memphis—where for years blacks and whites had co-existed peacefully, albeit somewhat uneasily, and had worked together to make genre-defining music—an epicenter of intolerance in the eyes of many.

The country was changing, and Elvis Presley, now an actor in frothy films rather than a snarling, swivel-hipped icon of rebellious youth, was starting to be seen as a quaint relic of a more innocent time. There was no denying that Elvis's stellar career, which two years in the army had done little to cool down, had begun to decline. His last number one hit, "Good Luck Charm," was in 1962. Each of the movies he had released since then—including *Kissin' Cousins*; *It Happened at the World's Fair*; *Clambake*; *Stay Away, Joe*; and *Live a Little, Love a Little*—had earned less than the one before it; the formula was getting old and the songs chosen for the sound tracks were getting worse. Elvis was truly embarrassed about some of the material, such as the scene in *Double Trouble* when he sings the children's song "Old MacDonald" and the lame attempt in *Girl Happy* to ignite a dance craze with "The Clam." The Colonel, who approved all the scripts, sometimes over Elvis's objections, was finding it harder and harder to get studios to pay the standard $1 million for an Elvis film. He was smart enough, however, to realize that something needed to be done to reignite interest in Elvis as a performer.

Parker's solution was a Christmas television special for NBC, Elvis's first TV appearance since Frank Sinatra's *Welcome Home Elvis* special in 1960. Plans for the program originally called for Elvis to fill the entire show by singing Christmas carols, but the director whom NBC attached to the project, Steve Binder, had more daring plans. He envisioned big sets, elaborate dance sequences, and lavish productions of Elvis's classic hits. Binder also wanted Elvis's input on the show, which made the singer very enthusiastic about taking part. The Colonel eventually came around to supporting the concept.

Binder had yet another idea, a novel one. He had watched Elvis and his band members in rehearsals, bantering and breaking into informal jam sessions. Binder thought that by putting a camera in these sessions, he could film interesting footage for the TV audience, who would get to see the King of Rock 'n' Roll in a more relaxed environment. Binder brought in Scotty Moore and D. J. Fontana, the two surviving members of Elvis's band from the Sun Studio days, to play, along with some Memphis Mafia buddies who were also musicians, Charlie Hodge, Alan Fortas, and Lance LeGault.

The only hitch in the plan was that even though the TV show would be prerecorded, Elvis had to perform live in front of an audience, something he had not done since 1961's benefit concert in Hawaii. After years of being isolated from his audience on movie lots and in recording studios, Elvis was not sure how the public would react to him. On June 29, the day of the live concert, Elvis was nearly overcome with a stage fright that he hadn't felt since his early days in the Memphis clubs. Sitting in the dressing room, after months of enthusiastic preparation and with an excited audience of four hundred waiting, Elvis told Binder he'd changed his mind; he could not go on. Panicked, Binder told him, "You get out there and save your career. If you won't do it for yourself, please do it for me."

The impassioned plea got through to Elvis, who nodded his head and made his way to the stage. The rest is TV and music history. Elvis not only overcame his trepidation about performing live but shook off whatever rust had accumulated on his performing skills and rocked the house.

The program, titled simply *Elvis* but known by fans as the '68 Comeback Special, aired on December 3, 1968. It opened with Elvis's rendition of the song "Guitar Man," an extended production number that functioned as a semiautobiographical minimovie, and included performances of his classic hits, including "That's All Right," "Heartbreak Hotel," "Love Me Tender," "Jailhouse Rock," and "Are You Lonesome Tonight?," as well as lesser-known songs such as "When My Blue Moon Turns to Gold Again" and "Lawdy Miss Clawdy." Elvis performed a medley of gospel songs as well as his signature Christmas song, "Blue Christmas." The Colonel was at first adamant that the show conclude with a holiday tune, but Elvis had a different idea for a show-closer. The song he chose was "If I Can Dream," a socially conscious ballad about peace and brotherhood written by Walter Earl Brown that included direct quotations from Martin Luther King, Jr. Elvis belted it out in a gospel-influenced style that evidenced raw and genuine emotion.

Elvis saw the song as his way to make a statement about the issues that defined the 1960s, which were some of the same issues that his own emergence on the national scene had stirred up in the 1950s. Unlike many celebrities today, Elvis strove throughout his career not to make overtly political statements. Nevertheless, he had been a lightning rod of controversy almost from the beginning. According to those who knew him well, he held no prejudices despite growing up in a very prejudiced time and place. Who could deny Elvis's love of black culture when it was all over his early recordings and when he himself on several occasions acknowledged rock 'n' roll's debt to the "Negro" genre of rhythm and blues? Historians today regard Elvis as the first artist to blend "black" and "white" music, in a sense becoming, himself, a symbol of racial harmony. Elvis desegregated music in the 1950s; in the 1960s, the rest of the country was painfully following suit.

Critics were nearly unanimous in their praise of the special, which is now regarded as a defining television moment of the decade. "Elvis Is Back" had already been used in 1960 as an album title, but this time it seemed that Elvis, at thirty-three, really was back.

As 1968 drew to a close, Elvis and those in his life had reason to celebrate the year, and they did so in a big way on New Year's Eve. Elvis rented the **(39) Thunderbird Lounge**, a hip nightclub at 750 Adams Street in the basement of the Shelborne Towers apartments, where he had spent the previous New Year's Eve. One of the hottest nightspots of the era, the Thunderbird, which opened in 1965, was one of several Memphis clubs established by nightlife impresario and former car salesman Ernie Barrasso. Barrasso had sold Elvis a Ford Thunderbird back in 1961, and Barrasso decided to parlay the publicity the sale had brought to him, the car, and the dealership into a new venture. He partnered with a liquor distributor to open the Thunderbird Lounge, which he named in honor of both the Ford automobile and the cheap wine that his partner was known for selling. The club was set up as two rooms (red and blue) with a dance floor and bar and became known for its live music, which included future stars such as Ronnie Milsap, Sam and Dave, and Charlie Rich. It drew a young professional crowd, despite its downscale, bring-your-own-liquor policy. Its success enabled Barrasso to open another club, Club Caesar, believed to be Memphis's first discotheque, in 1967. Like Elvis, Barrasso was a regular traveler to Vegas, and Club Caesar's Roman-inspired décor, complete with toga-clad staff, came from the then-new Caesar's Palace.

Barrasso became known as Memphis's "Disco King," but on New Year's Eve 1968, there was only one King in the Thunderbird Lounge—and he believed that he had reclaimed his throne.

♫♫♫♫

by the way

a shot heard 'round the world

Doting on their new child and still in newlywed bliss, Elvis and Priscilla seemed happy in their own world in the spring of 1968. However, on the civil rights front, things had gotten even worse in Memphis and were about to escalate into one of the decade's most devastating tragedies.

The Lorraine Motel, at 406 Mulberry Street at Huling Avenue—about a half-mile south of Beale Street—had long been known as the most welcoming establishment in town for African American customers. Nat King Cole and Sarah Vaughan once stayed there, and in the 1960s, the Lorraine became a hangout for both black and white musicians. Otis Redding, Wilson Pickett, and Eddie Floyd cooled down in the motel's swimming pool after long days recording in the non-air-conditioned facilities of Stax Records nearby. The fact that the Lorraine was a symbol of racial harmony in a city still struggling with its segregationist past was probably what made it appeal to the Reverend Martin Luther King, Jr. The civil rights leader stayed there regularly in Room 306, down the hall from where Pickett and Steve Cropper wrote "In the Midnight Hour."

On April 4, 1968, King was in Memphis to lend his support to a gathering of black sanitation workers who were striking to protest what they considered a pattern of workplace discrimination and unsafe working conditions. The strike, which started on February 11, inflamed racial tensions in the city. During King's previous visit to Memphis, on March 28, during which he had hoped to lead a peaceful march, events descended into chaos, with looting and rioting in the streets and police resorting to using mace and tear gas to control the massive crowd of strikers and their supporters. This time, the city was taking no chances; it brought in National Guard troops to patrol the streets in anticipation of more violence and civil disobedience and imposed martial law throughout the city. Because of the Lorraine's exposed balconies, King's aides wanted him to stay at the more secure Peabody, but the reverend stuck with his usual room at the Lorraine so as not to be branded a hypocrite by African Americans. Shortly after 6:00 p.m., he was standing outside his room, dressed for dinner, when James Earl Ray fired the shots that killed him.

Today, a white wreath marks the spot where King died. The Lorraine, which went bankrupt in 1982 after years of neighborhood economic decline, put its historic infamy to good use when a group of Memphis businessmen took it over; in 1992, it reopened as the National Civil Rights Museum, a shrine to King and his dream of civil rights for all through nonviolent means. It is now a popular, if solemn, stop on the itinerary of many Memphis visitors.

Elvis and his buddies were regulars at the Arcade, Memphis's oldest café. A plaque inside marks Elvis's favorite booth.

The Stax Museum of American Soul Music stands on the site of the Stax recording studio, where Elvis made his 1975 album *Promised Land*.

Elvis performing in the 1970s.

chapter 7

downward spiral

The end of the 1960s brought tough times for both Elvis Presley and the city of Memphis. The assassination of Martin Luther King marked the beginning of Memphis's social and economic deterioration, which would linger into the 1980s. In a sad reversal of fortune, the city once known for groundbreaking music that married white and black cultural influences was now infamous as the city that killed the nation's greatest voice for racial equality and harmony. In the 1950s, people flocked to Memphis to take a shot at their dreams; just a few years later, people were leaving in droves. Middle-class whites fled to the suburbs, while the less mobile, more impoverished black population stayed put in the inner city. It was a recipe for economic decline and rising crime. People and businesses no longer felt safe, and many of those that didn't relocate simply faded away. The Peabody, the Chisca, the original Lansky Brothers Clothiers, and numerous Beale Street clubs and restaurants were among the many establishments that were claimed, either temporarily or permanently, by the decay.

The deterioration of Elvis's personal life mirrored that of Memphis, although his career had one more great run left that would lead him back to Las Vegas—but only after one more Memphis milestone.

hits from the ghetto

In January 1969, Elvis recorded in Memphis for the first time since 1955. The sessions took place at **(40) American Sound Studio**, a tiny building at 827 Thomas Street, in the middle of a poor, run-down, mostly black area of North Memphis. The studio was founded in 1965 by Lincoln "Chips" Moman, who had produced some of the first hits for Satellite Records (later known as Stax Records) but severed his ties with the company after a monetary dispute. Moman always used the same rhythm group, called the Memphis Boys (or, alternatively, the 827 Thomas Street Band), to back up the various artists he recorded, creating the studio's distinctive sound.

American Sound Studio helped to establish what is now known as the "Memphis sound," a style mostly associated with the genre of soul music. When the Brits started taking over rock 'n' roll in the mid-1960s, followed by the influence of the drug culture on the sound of rock, Memphis's recording studios went back to their "race music" roots, once again blending elements of gospel and blues for a style that was nationally popular but had a distinct regional flavor. The Memphis sound is characterized by deep bass lines; light guitar; keys; strong, soulful R&B-type vocals; and a powerful driving drum beat, often also with horns. Aretha Franklin, Isaac Hayes, Sam and Dave, and Al Green are among the artists whose work from the mid-1960s through mid-1970s reflects this style. Elvis surely felt more affinity for the Memphis sound than he did for the psychedelic-influenced rock music of the time.

The two Elvis albums that came from the American Sound sessions—*From Elvis in Memphis* and *Back in Memphis*—represent a creative high point in Elvis's career. They were the first studio albums after years of nothing but movie sound tracks, which both Elvis and his fans knew had become stale. The albums produced four hit singles in 1969 and 1970: "In the Ghetto," "Suspicious Minds," "Don't Cry Daddy," and "Kentucky Rain."

American Sound Studio was literally in the ghetto: the neighborhood was so rough that guard dogs patrolled the area around the building, and an armed guard was stationed on the roof to prevent crime in the parking lot. Despite its location, it drew famous artists to its facilities; American Sound produced more than a hundred Top 40 hits. Besides the singles from Elvis's two albums recorded there, these included Neil Diamond's "Sweet Caroline," Dusty Springfield's "Son of a Preacher Man," B. J. Thomas's "Hooked on a Feeling" and "Raindrops Keep Falling on My Head," and the Box Tops' "The Letter."

American Sound Studio's reign at the top was brief: it closed in 1972, and a parking lot now marks the spot where so many great singles—and Elvis Presley's last great albums—were recorded.

sin city redux

Elvis filmed his last movie in 1969: *Change of Habit,* which was part of the deal the Colonel had made with NBC to produce the '68 Comeback Special. In perhaps his oddest role, Elvis portrayed a hip young doctor who works at an inner-city clinic with a nun played by Mary Tyler Moore. However, even as his screen acting career faded, Elvis was re-embarking on a career as a live musical performer. In July 1969, he was booked for an extended engagement at the newly built International Hotel in Las Vegas, which boasted the city's largest show-room. Elvis put together a huge, crowd-pleasing production, with an orchestra, a rock band, and assorted male and female gospel backup singers. He sported karate-inspired outfits for his shows, at first simple two-piece black or white ensembles. As time went on, these evolved into one-piece jumpsuits that got flashier and more ornate, sometimes incorporating capes. He began making an epic, bombastic stage entrance to the opening bars of Richard Strauss's *Thus Spake Zarathustra,* a piece that had recently become well-known through its use in Stanley Kubrick's science fiction film *2001: A Space Odyssey.*

Elvis's opening night was a major show-business event, with celebrities such as Fats Domino, Dick Clark, Angie Dickinson, George Hamilton, Ann-Margret, Wayne ("Mr. Las Vegas") Newton, and Sam Phillips, who was personally invited by Elvis, in attendance. The Elvis

Presley show at the International was the hottest ticket in Vegas, and the experience was so invigorating to Elvis that, by the end of the first engagement, he was ready to start touring on a regular basis. For the next seven years, in a complete turnaround from the previous decade, live concert performances, rather than movies, were Elvis's (and the Colonel's) bread and butter.

Although Elvis was happy to no longer be making mediocre movies, his feelings about the fading of his acting career were bittersweet. He never gave up his dream of being recognized as a serious actor and even took a stab at being a filmmaker. In 1974, he began work on a movie project of his own, a documentary about karate called *The New Gladiators*, with his martial arts mentor, Ed Parker. Elvis was to be the producer, star, and narrator of the film, which would follow karate students from training through tournament competition. Unfortunately, although some footage was shot, Elvis never finished the project.

mr. presley and mr. president

Elvis had developed a fascination with police work, badges, and guns. He was proud of his collection of honorary badges from law enforcement organizations across the country. As for guns, he not only collected them; he liked carrying and using them. Stories abound of Elvis and his friends' reckless gunplay. On at least one occasion, after an anonymous death threat, Elvis packed heat onstage, tucking a derringer into his boot and a .45 into his waistband. His obsession with security—which extended to installing closed-circuit cameras in and around his home—sprang from both legitimate fears in the wake of the Manson family murders in 1969 and an increasing paranoia brought on by drug use.

Elvis's biggest coup as a collector of law-enforcement memorabilia came on December 21, 1970. Despite his own abuse of drugs, he was a harsh and public critic of the drug culture that had taken hold among America's youth. He drafted a letter to President Richard Nixon offering his services in America's war on drugs in exchange for official federal credentials. Elvis flew to Washington, D.C., with body-guard Jerry Schilling to present the handwritten letter personally. The awestruck guards at the White House's northwest gate took the letter to Nixon's staff. Nixon agreed not only to meet with Elvis on short notice but to award him a badge and photo ID naming him a "special assistant" in the Bureau of Narcotics and Dangerous Drugs. The photo taken at the conclusion of this Oval Office meeting—with Elvis in a purple crushed-velvet suit and cape and huge gold belt shaking hands with the famously dour president in his gray suit—has become one of the era's iconic images. Elvis was proud of this honor, though many of those around him could only snicker at the supreme irony of Elvis, by now a veritable walking pharmacy, playing the role of an enforcer of drug laws.

About a month later, Elvis received another honor when the Jaycees named him one of the Ten Outstanding Young Men of the Year, an award granted to men under thirty-five who had distinguished themselves in their chosen fields. The awards ceremony took place in Memphis, which meant that Elvis, as the hometown boy, could play the gracious host, inviting his fellow recipients and the hosts to Graceland for cocktails, followed by a formal, elegant dinner at the **(41) Four Flames**, a popular midtown restaurant at 1085 Poplar Avenue. It was known for its four flaming desserts—bananas Foster, cherries jubilee, crêpes Suzette, and baked Alaska. Today, the Patton-Bejach House, the nineteenth-century Victorian building that housed the Four Flames, is listed on the National Register of Historic Places and serves as the headquarters of Memphis's Child Advocacy Center.

separate ways

Elvis went into an RCA recording studio in Los Angeles in March 1972 to record material for a new album, a session that yielded his last Top 10 hit, "Burning Love," a bouncy, energetic tune written by Dennis Linde that is regarded by many as Elvis's last true rock 'n' roll song. Still a crowd-pleaser when performed today by Elvis cover artists and other performers, the song was not one of Elvis's favorites. By early 1972, the man who had once symbolized rock 'n' roll was moving away from rock 'n' roll, more interested in bittersweet, melancholy ballads such as "For the Good Times" (written by Kris Kristofferson) and "Always on My Mind," both of which were more memorably performed by country-and-western artists (Ray Price and Willie Nelson, respectively). The reason, undoubtedly, had to do with the emotional blow he had suffered in his private life: Priscilla left him after five years of marriage.

The resurgence of Elvis's touring career—and the travel, long nights, and temptations that came with it—could not be reconciled with the demands of his marriage. On February 23, 1972, Elvis and Priscilla legally separated, and Elvis filed for divorce in August of that year. The divorce became final on October 9, 1973, with Elvis maintaining joint legal custody of Lisa Marie.

The reasons for the split were many and varied, on both sides. For Priscilla, they ranged from Elvis's long absences from home to his increasingly out-of-control drug use and rumored womanizing, to a disturbing lack of intimacy after the birth of their daughter. It has been alleged that Elvis never made love to Priscilla after Lisa Marie was born and had a hang-up about having sex with anyone who'd had a child. As for Elvis, he was driven mad by jealousy (which turned out to be justified) over Priscilla's affair with a dance instructor and, later, over her relationship with a karate instructor whom Elvis had recommended to her, Mike Stone. Thus did Elvis's attempts to include his wife in his eclectic hobbies, like martial arts training, ultimately backfire. The haunting refrain of Elvis's recent number one hit was sadly prophetic: "We can't go on together . . . with suspicious minds."

nights on the town

With Priscilla and Lisa Marie no longer part of his daily life, Elvis was a man without an anchor, untethered to any of the responsibilities of husband and father that had put a slight damper on his increasingly reckless lifestyle. His dependence on drugs was getting worse, causing mood swings and other erratic behavior; his body, which had made women swoon in the 1950s when he swiveled his hips, was beginning to show the effects of overindulgent eating. Memphis is a town known for barbecue and other heavy, calorie-laden food, and Elvis notoriously loved his hometown cuisine. His eating habits were a contributing factor to the poor health that plagued him in the 1970s.

The newly single Elvis reacted to his situation as one might expect given his lifelong habits. He spent more time with the Memphis Mafia, many of whom had become as addicted as Elvis—not just to the pills to which they had easy access thanks to their boss and Dr. Nick, but to the celebrity lifestyle itself. Yet when they were in Memphis, they were treated like the local boys made good that most of them were. Among their traditions were late-night dinners at the **(42) Gridiron** restaurant, located at what is now 4101 Elvis Presley Boulevard, a twenty-four-hour restaurant down the street from Graceland. Cheeseburgers were among Elvis's favorite foods and he especially liked the ones at the Gridiron, which came with lettuce, tomato, and onion on the side. Another hangout was **(43) Coletta's**, an Italian restaurant at 1063 South Parkway East that claims to be both Memphis's oldest restaurant (it dates to 1923) and the originator of barbecue pizza, one of Elvis's favorite meals. In addition to the original location, which served Elvis and the Memphis Mafia, a second Coletta's is at 2850 Appling Road.

There were new girlfriends in the picture before too long. One of them was another Memphis native, model and actress Cybill Shepherd. Shepherd, who had won the Miss Teenage Memphis contest in 1966, came to national attention in 1971's *The Last Picture Show*, directed by Peter Bogdanovich. She and Elvis were said to have had a very intimate and physical relationship, but according to Shepherd's autobiography, Elvis's drug use ultimately pushed her away—into the arms of Bogdanovich, whom she dated through much of the 1970s. Shepherd became a big Hollywood star in the 1970s and 1980s but retained close ties to Memphis, even moving back for a while in 1978 and marrying a local auto parts dealer, David Ford. Known for her political activism, she helped fund the National Civil Rights Museum.

Elvis had a more lasting relationship with Linda Thompson, also from Memphis, an aspiring actress and songwriter who shared Elvis's love of gospel music. She and Elvis met at an event at the Memphian Theater in July 1972; Linda moved into Graceland shortly thereafter. She was Elvis's steady girlfriend for more than three years, staying by his side through some very trying times.

trouble on tour

Elvis was bigger than ever in the 1970s, and not just in the literal sense. In his now nearly constant touring, he played some of the country's largest venues—the Houston Astrodome in 1970, Lake Tahoe in 1971, New York's Madison Square Garden in 1972, and, that same year, Honolulu's International Convention Center Arena for the *Aloha from Hawaii* concert. On New Year's Eve 1975, he performed in Detroit's Pontiac Silverdome, setting a single-performance attendance record of 62,500.

In between the stadium appearances were numerous engagements in Las Vegas, particularly at the Hilton Hotel. One rumor (never confirmed) was that Elvis was doing so many shows in Vegas because the Colonel, reputed to be a big-time gambler, had racked up immense gambling debts at the Hilton, and the performances were part of his deal to pay them back. Elvis, now approaching forty, was living life at a frenetic pace. Larry Geller, one of Elvis's closest confidants in his later years, believed that the primary reason for Elvis's drug addiction and poor diet, and the weight gain that came with them, was the brutal performance schedule. The Colonel, Geller believed, was running his star into the ground.

Elvis may have agreed. In October 1973, Elvis was admitted to Baptist Memorial Hospital, where he was treated for pneumonia, pleurisy, hepatitis, and an enlarged colon. He was hospitalized there again in January 1975 for severe physical pain and canceled several shows that January and February. During this stay, the doctors tried to wean him off the various medications he was taking, but those efforts were not successful. Colonel Parker was irked about the canceled engagements, but there was little he could do about them. Similarly, no one could stop Elvis from self-medicating in prodigious amounts; Vernon, his father (and de facto financial manager), could not stop him from spending lavishly on cars, jewelry, and airplanes; and neither the Colonel nor anyone at RCA could make him stick to a recording schedule.

the heart of soul

Eventually, however, despite the toll that the divorce, the touring, and his health problems were exacting from him, Elvis had to take his commitment to his record label seriously. RCA needed material for a new album in the summer of 1973, and the studio where Elvis chose to record it was a Memphis music-biz institution that was to soul music what Sun Records was to early rock 'n' roll: **(44) Stax Records**, at 926 East McLemore Avenue, just down the street from Elvis's old church, First Baptist, and today the site of the Stax Museum of American Soul Music.

Founded in a garage in 1957 as Satellite Records, Stax Records originally put out country and pop records by white artists, reflecting the taste of its founder, Jim Stewart. Shortly after releasing the R&B hit "'Cause I Love You," by the Memphis-based duo of Rufus Thomas and his daughter Carla in 1961, Satellite became Stax and set up shop in the old Capitol movie theater on McLemore. Stewart's sister, Estelle Axton, joined the business (hence the name "Stax," which combines their two surnames), and the two, along with Chips Moman, concentrated on recording and promoting the emerging black stars of R&B, jazz, blues, and, eventually, the styles that would come to be known as funk and soul. The artists who recorded at Stax—for the Stax label itself, for one of its various subsidiary labels such as Volt, or for the larger Atlantic label with which Stax had a distribution deal—range from house band

Booker T. and the MG's, to Otis Redding, Isaac Hayes, the Staple Singers, and Sam and Dave, to pioneering black comics such as Bill Cosby and Richard Pryor.

Stax came upon hard times in the mid-1970s and went bankrupt in 1975. It was resurrected chiefly as a reissue label in the late 1970s. The studio building was torn down in 1989; the museum, designed as a replica of the original studio, opened to the public in 2003. Because Stax's connection to Elvis's career is somewhat peripheral, only a few Elvis mementos are on display, but anyone intrigued by Memphis's musical history will find many items of interest, including Isaac Hayes's restored, peacock-blue "Superfly" Cadillac Eldorado, a gold-sequined dress worn onstage by Tina Turner, and a saxophone recovered from the crash that killed Otis Redding.

Although Elvis was not known as a Stax artist, he did record three albums at the Stax studio in 1973—*Raised on Rock*, *Good Times*, and *Promised Land*. With these recordings, he had left his musical footprint at every major recording studio in Memphis.

bonding with the swami

The Memphis Mafia continued to grow in number, until what had started as a close-knit coterie of Elvis's cousins, high school friends, and army buddies had become a huge entourage that included Dr. Nick; Lowell Hays, Elvis's official jeweler; and Master Kang Rhee, his karate instructor. The one who was closest to Elvis at this point in his life, however, was Larry Geller, who had left the fold in 1967 over conflicts with some of the members of the Memphis Mafia and with Priscilla but returned in the 1970s at Elvis's request.

Geller's return was greeted with annoyance by the many in Elvis's inner circle who disliked and distrusted him, and they often derogatorily referred to Geller as "the swami." To Elvis, however, Geller was something of a guru. He was a well-known Hollywood hairdresser when he met Elvis in 1964, having worked with Paul Newman, Steve

McQueen, and Warren Beatty. Elvis and Geller bonded almost instantly. Elvis was enraptured by Geller's talks on meditation, yoga, vegetarianism, and various spiritual issues. Naturally inquisitive, Elvis turned to Geller frequently throughout the next few years, hoping to take his mind off the drudgery of making movies that embarrassed him. From these conversations, Elvis developed an intense interest in New Age spirituality and world religions, another hobby that he would pursue almost to obsession, along with karate, guns, and police badges. Elvis's other friends, and even Priscilla, grew to resent the influence Geller exerted on Elvis. Geller's ouster from the inner circle occurred shortly after Elvis's marriage to Priscilla.

Elvis trusted Geller with secrets that he shared with few others. According to Geller, toward the end, Elvis was ready for a change in his life and career—he was planning to fire the Colonel, improve his diet and get off the pills, and find some good dramatic movie roles to prove that he could really act. But more than good intentions were necessary to break the cycle in which Elvis was trapped. He did attempt to fire the Colonel after a particularly heated blowup over canceled shows and recording sessions in August 1973, but after several uncomfortable days and a realistic look at the finances with Vernon, Elvis realized that, for better or worse, he and the Colonel needed each other.

taking care of business

Two Memphis jewelers were associated with Elvis Presley. One was Levitch, who sold him his wedding bands. The other was Lowell Hays, who basically made a career out of supplying Elvis with jewelry. Hays was responsible for crafting the first pieces of jewelry that bore the logo of Elvis and the Memphis Mafia, a stylized lightning bolt with the initials "TCB." The initials stood for the motto that Elvis and his crew had adopted, "Taking care of business." As for the origin of the logo's design, it depends on whom you ask; as with much Elvis lore, there are conflicting accounts. Some say Priscilla designed it; others say the lightning bolt was based on a symbol of the actual mafia. Another theory is that the lightning bolt was based on the insignia of Elvis's army battalion. Yet another is that the lightning bolt was modeled after the logo of Elvis's favorite comic book hero, Captain Marvel. Kathy Westmoreland, who sang backup vocals for Elvis's shows in 1970 and dated him briefly while he and Priscilla were separated, claims that Elvis told her he got the idea from a bolt of lightning that left a pattern on a marble statue—a sign from God, he believed. Whatever the story, Hays was the jeweler who crafted much of the TCB jewelry; the pendants, in particular, were coveted items among the Presley faithful, because receiving one was the ultimate sign of Elvis's friendship and trust—the unmistakable badge of Memphis Mafia membership.

The **(45) Lowell Hays and Sons** jewelry store (4872 Poplar Avenue), a family business, started in 1937, with Hays's father, Lowell Hays, Sr., doing jewelry repair work out of his Memphis home. By 1943, his business had grown, and he set up shop in an office at Main Street and Union Avenue. Hays, Jr., joined the business in 1961, and the father-son team opened their first retail store on South Perkins Road in 1971.

It was around this time that Hays, Jr., met Elvis. The two hit it off instantly. Hays soon became known as Elvis's personal jeweler, often traveling with him and the rest of the entourage on tours. The briefcase full of jewelry that Hays toted with him became nearly as vital to the touring entourage as Dr. Nick's medical bag, at the ready in the increasingly likely event that Elvis would decide on a whim to buy someone a shiny new gift. Hays counted other musicians, including Isaac Hayes, Al Green, T. G. Sheppard, and the members of the band Alabama, as his clients. He retired in 2006, closing the store that had become a Memphis institution, though he still sells jewelry on his website, www .elvisjeweler.com.

The TCB logo was also used in a patch on Elvis's karate uniform that was designed by Elvis and his karate instructor, Master Kang Rhee. Kang Rhee still runs a martial arts training studio near Memphis: the **(46) Kang Rhee Institute**, 706 Germantown Parkway #70, in the suburban community of Cordova, northeast of Memphis.

Nowadays, many casual Elvis fans dismiss Elvis's karate moves onstage as shtick or showmanship. But Elvis was a very serious student of the martial arts, and he is honored in the Martial Arts Hall of Fame along with Chuck Norris, Jackie Chan, and Bruce Lee.

By the time he met Kang Rhee in 1970, Elvis had been studying karate for more than a decade. When he returned from the army, he made the acquaintance of Ed Parker, regarded as the father of the American *kenpo* style, who encouraged Elvis to continue the training he had begun under Juergen Seydel in Germany and go for his black belt. Elvis accomplished this milestone in 1960 under an instructor recommended by Parker, Hank Slomanski.

Parker also recommended Kang Rhee, a former Korean grand champion, who instructed Elvis from 1970 through 1974 and promoted him to seventh-degree black belt in 1973. That same year, Elvis gave Kang Rhee a car—a slightly used white Cadillac Eldorado that Vernon had customized as a gift for his son—to show his enormous gratitude to his teacher. Elvis received his eighth-degree black belt certificate from Rhee on September 16, 1974, in a low-key, private ceremony that Elvis surely appreciated now that his celebrity had made such quiet gatherings nearly impossible.

the last tour

The extent of Elvis's declining physical and emotional health was evident during his later tours, including his final live performances in Memphis, several of which occurred at the **(47) Mid-South Coliseum** at 996 Early Maxwell Boulevard. The 10,085-seat multipurpose coliseum was built in 1963 primarily to serve as a hockey arena for the Memphis Wings of the old Central Hockey League. It originally had piping installed beneath the floor that was used to cover the floor with ice for games; at other times, Memphis residents used the arena for ice skating. Later on, the coliseum became the home of three Memphis basketball teams that played in the American Basketball Association from 1971 to 1975. Like Ellis Auditorium, it was a popular venue for professional wrestling, serving as home base for the United States Wrestling Association and hosting numerous matches featuring Memphis native Jerry "The King" Lawler. The Coliseum hosted numerous concerts, sporting events, and shows until it closed in 2006.

The Mid-South Coliseum staked a claim in music history as one of the few stops on the Beatles' last American tour in 1966. The group played two shows there in August; during one, an audience member exploded a firecracker. Many in the nervous crowd, who had been expecting trouble from the Ku Klux Klan in response to John Lennon's recent, controversial statement that the Beatles were bigger than Jesus, mistook the sound for a gunshot. The resulting pandemonium alarmed the band, and the only Beatle to ever return was George Harrison, in 1974, the same year that Elvis played his first show there. Elvis's performance took place on March 20 of that year and was recorded for the album *Recorded Live on Stage in Memphis*.

Elvis returned for a several-night engagement in 1975. During his June 10 show, the heavy but still energetic Elvis endured the on-stage embarrassment of splitting the seat of his pants when he bent over to kiss a female fan. He treated the incident with good humor, and the reviews of the show were mostly positive, but everyone around him knew that the weight gain was becoming bad not only for his image but also for his health. Elvis's final concert in Memphis took place at the Coliseum in front of an audience of 12,000 on July 5, 1976—twenty-two years to the day after he had recorded "That's All Right" in Sam Phillips's little recording studio. His last live show was in Indianapolis, at the Indiana Market Square Arena, on June 26, 1977.

romance and betrayal

Elvis's romance with Linda Thompson ended in 1976. Elvis had seemingly lost interest in sex altogether, a trait that some have attributed to his heavy drug use as well as his growing obsession with spiritual matters. In late 1976, Ginger Alden—a dark-haired, Memphis-born actress who had met Elvis back in 1960, when she was five years old—re-entered his life. On November 19, George Klein arranged a meeting between Elvis and the current Miss Tennessee—Ginger's older sister, Terry—with the intention of setting up the two. However, Elvis was instantly attracted to the younger sister. Despite the age difference, Elvis and Ginger swiftly became a couple. As with Priscilla, many in the Memphis Mafia distrusted her and resented her demands on Elvis's time. Ginger had the distinction of being the last serious girlfriend of Elvis's life—and the last one to see him alive. Ginger claims that the two were engaged to be married at the time of his death.

A turning point in Elvis's relationship with his inner circle occurred in July 1976, when three of Elvis's bodyguards—Red West, Sonny West, and Dave Hebler—were fired by Vernon, who was irked about the amount of money his son was spending to keep his friends employed. Embittered, the three men decided to get back at their former friend by writing a tell-all book. They took their stories to journalist Steve Dunleavy, who compiled them into the unauthorized biography *Elvis: What Happened?* The book was the first to reveal salacious details about Elvis's affairs, fits of anger, sexual peculiarities, and—perhaps most shocking to his faithful fans—abuse of drugs. The underlying message of the story that his three longtime friends were telling was that Elvis was slowly killing himself with drugs. Although critics of the book point out various factual errors, there was no question that the book was severely damaging to Elvis's reputation.

When Elvis heard about the book, and learned how he was portrayed in it, he was enraged. His mood swings had become extreme, and he suffered from dark moments in which he would tell his friends about plots he had hatched to kill Sonny, Red, and Dave. He had already spoken of hiring a hit man to kill Mike Stone, the man whom he blamed for Priscilla's leaving him. Fortunately, he never followed up on any of these threats.

His friends' betrayal should have served as a wake-up call to Elvis, but it did not, nor did yet another stay in a Memphis hospital in April 1977, brought on by exhaustion and severe gastric problems.

More shows were canceled, and the shows that Elvis did perform around this time reflected his physical and emotional decline.

roller-coaster ride

Time and economic conditions have claimed the place where Elvis was last seen alive in public. On August 7, 1977, Elvis rented out **(48) Libertyland**, 940 Early Maxwell Boulevard, the amusement park at Memphis's Mid-South Fairgrounds. Among Libertyland's twenty-four rides and attractions was Elvis's favorite roller coaster, the Zippin Pippin, which he rode that night for hours without a break.

The Zippin Pippin, originally just called the Pippin, was a piece of Memphis history. One of the oldest wooden roller coasters in the United States, the Pippin was constructed around 1912 (some accounts place the date in 1915 or 1917) by a company called National Amusement Devices and was originally situated in Memphis's East End Park. Its frame was made of pine; the track was 2,865 feet long, with a drop of 70 feet. The 90-second ride had a maximum speed of 40 miles per hour. As East End Park declined in popularity, the coaster was moved to the horse track in Montgomery Park, which became the Mid-South Fairgrounds, and was an attraction at the fairs there until the city of Memphis decided to build the bicentennial-themed Libertyland around it in the 1970s. The "Zippin" was added to the coaster's name for the opening of the park, and the historic ride was one of the signature attractions, along with another classic ride, the Grand Carousel, and newer ones such as the Revolution, a steel coaster; the Tidal Wave, a topspin ride; and the Rebellion, a tower with a 90-foot drop.

Financial difficulties forced Libertyland to close in 2005. The public land that made up the Mid-South Fairgrounds was gradually sold off to private developers, and the Zippin Pippin was sold at auction in 2010 after several changes in ownership. At one point, Dolly Parton's Dollywood expressed an interest in acquiring it, but it ended up in Green Bay, Wisconsin, at that city's Bay Beach Amusement Park.

Who knows what was going through Elvis's troubled mind that night as he rode the coaster over and over with his friends? He had come so far from the days of his youth; perhaps he wanted to recapture the innocence, anonymity, and carefree abandon of the early days. His evolution—from poor Memphis kid to local singing sensation to national star to living legend to almost caricature of himself—was now complete. Meanwhile, the city where he grew up and had became a star was becoming more and more unrecognizable, many places from his youth either boarded up or slowly dying. The innocence of the past was out of reach, and the future was more uncertain than ever.

end of the road

That future, as it turned out, was tragically brief. On August 16, 1977, shortly after midnight, Elvis returned to Graceland from a late-night trip to his dentist, Dr. Lester Hofman, who, like all of Elvis's retinue, was on call twenty-four hours a day. After preparing throughout the early-morning hours for a tour scheduled to begin the next day in Portland, Maine, Elvis retired to the master bedroom at about 7:00 a.m. to rest up for his flight that evening. Ginger, who was staying with him, woke up at about 1:30 in the afternoon and realized that Elvis had not come back to bed after going to the bathroom several hours before. She knocked on Elvis's bathroom door; after hearing no response, she pushed it open.

Ginger was shocked to see Elvis lying facedown in a pool of vomit on the floor, pajama bottoms around his ankles. He had fallen off the toilet and was not moving or breathing. Frantically, Ginger called the maid at Graceland, who got the word to one of Elvis's bodyguards, Al Strada. Strada phoned for an ambulance. Joe Esposito and Charlie Hodge charged up the stairs to the bedroom to perform CPR. Friends and family arrived in waves, and the mansion became a scene of utter chaos. Vernon desperately begged, "Please, son, don't go, please don't die." Nine-year-old Lisa Marie, who was visiting for a few weeks before Elvis's tour began, came upon the scene, asking, "What's wrong with my daddy?" before the adults locked the doors to spare her the gruesome tableau. EMTs arrived from a nearby firehouse and loaded Elvis onto a stretcher, though it was obvious to most that nothing could be done; his vital signs were nonexistent. Dr. Nick, Joe, and Charlie rode with Elvis in the ambulance, Dr. Nick desperately trying to revive Elvis. The ambulance arrived at Baptist Memorial Hospital around 3:00. Elvis was declared dead at 3:30.

The cause of death was listed as cardiac arrhythmia, medical terminology for a type of heart condition, and the initial reports pointed to some sort of cardiovascular disease. The real story, painstakingly covered up for years by Elvis's family and handlers, had more to do with the deadly combination of drugs in his system: the painkillers morphine and Demerol; the antihistamine chlorpheniramine; the tranquilizers Placidyl and Valium; and traces of codeine, quaaludes, and barbiturates. At the time of his death, Elvis weighed more than 250 pounds, and his heart was grotesquely enlarged.

farewell to a legend

The sordid details of Elvis's final days and the murky facts behind the cause of his death were far from the minds of most of the mourners at his huge public funeral. At Vernon's insistence, the viewing and the service took place at Graceland so fans could see Elvis one last time. On August 17, the day of the viewing, as many as 50,000 people gathered outside the gates of the mansion—some even climbed trees to get a better view—to watch Elvis's copper casket, carried in a long white hearse preceded by a motorcycle escort, borne up the front steps into the living room. With his hair and makeup supervised by his friend Geller, Elvis looked youthful and handsome.

For the first time in years, the eyes of the nation—and indeed the world—were on Memphis, Tennessee. When the family opened the doors of Graceland for the public viewing, it was as if an entire country was converging on the estate to grieve. One hundred vans transported the thousands of floral displays sent by grieving fans. National

Guardsmen were called in to assist the Memphis police with crowd control. Mourners fainted while waiting in line in the Memphis heat. By the time the gates to Graceland finally closed, thousands had said their farewells to the King of Rock 'n' Roll. Later that evening, at a smaller, private wake, those closest to Elvis and a handful of famous admirers, including Priscilla, soul singer James Brown, and Caroline Kennedy, paid their respects.

Joe Esposito and Vernon lined up some of Elvis's favorite gospel singers—J. D. Sumner and the Stamps, Jake Hess, James Blackwood—to perform at the private service. Colonel Parker did not view the body, instead choosing to engage the grieving Vernon in an intense conversation about the future, specifically how to protect Elvis's legacy from exploitation.

Like his mother, Elvis was buried in Forest Hill Cemetery; both were later moved to the grounds of Graceland and reburied in the meditation garden that had offered Elvis solace when he was alive. His headstone stands alongside those of Gladys, Vernon, and his grandmother Minnie Mae. His stillborn twin brother, Jesse Garon, whose remains are buried in an unmarked grave in Tupelo, is commemorated by a small marker. The garden is strewn with tributes from fans from around the world.

Vernon Presley leaves a flower at Elvis's grave in the meditation garden at Graceland. Thousands of Elvis fans have visited the grave since the King's death in 1977.

epilogue

the king is dead, long live the king

"**E**lvis Presley is worth more dead than he ever was alive." So goes the cliché; it may very well be true. The cottage industry that sprang up—and continues to thrive—in the wake of Elvis's death in 1977 is unprecedented and unmatched by that around any celebrity before or since. Perhaps even more important, Elvis's death served as a catalyst for the revitalization of the city of Memphis. The watershed moment for both of these phenomena was Graceland's transformation from private home to museum. And yet, it nearly didn't happen.

The foundations for the future earnings of Elvis's estate were laid as early as 1954 by Bob Neal, his first manager, who set up Elvis Presley Enterprises to profit from Elvis-related merchandise. The organization ceased to exist when the Colonel took over Elvis's management, but it was reestablished under the Elvis Presley Trust, set up in Elvis's will, which took over his assets after his death. Vernon, Minnie Mae, and Lisa Marie were the beneficiaries of the trust; Vernon became the executor after his son's death. However, Vernon died only two years later, and Minnie Mae a year after that, leaving Lisa Marie the sole heir.

Priscilla, Lisa Marie's legal guardian, became a trustee after Vernon's death and at first was inclined to let Parker continue to handle the business affairs of her ex-husband's estate. However, after speaking to the court-appointed lawyer who investigated Parker's management due to Lisa Marie's minor status, Priscilla was shocked to learn the extent to which Parker's financial shenanigans and Elvis's years of profligate spending had put her daughter's inheritance in jeopardy. By the time of Elvis's death, Parker had managed to negotiate a contract that paid him no less than 50 percent of Elvis's earnings. Parker had also made an ill-advised deal in 1973 wherein he sold to RCA the rights to all the royalties from all of Elvis's songs prior to that year. The court investigating Parker's management ruled the 50 percent rate "extortionate" and the RCA sale "unethical." On top of that, Elvis's estate owed $15 million in back taxes. Several years of courtroom wrangling followed. Elvis Presley Enterprises (EPE), led by Priscilla, sued Parker for mismanagement; Parker countersued. The result was an out-of-court settlement that resulted in Parker's terminating his association with the estate for five years and handing over to the estate all the recordings and photos he owned at the time. (Parker reestablished friendly relations with the estate in later years.)

The upkeep of Graceland, which was bequeathed to Lisa Marie in Elvis's will, cost about $500,000 per year. With the IRS still nipping at the estate's heels, Priscilla was advised to sell the property to avoid bankruptcy. Instead, she decided to turn the house into a museum, and Graceland opened to the public on June 7, 1982. In subsequent years, EPE would buy up much of the property across the street from the mansion and take over the merchandise shops (originally opened by bootleggers) that had sprung up there. The Heartbreak Hotel, also operated by EPE, opened in 1999. Lisa Marie Presley joined the management team of EPE in 1998 and served as chairman of the board until 2005; today she owns Graceland outright, as well as 15 percent of EPE; the other

85 percent of EPE is owned by billionaire Robert Sillerman, who acquired it in 2005.

Graceland's transformation into a tourist destination not only lured hordes of the King's avid fans to Memphis, a city that many had given up for dead but also firmly established Elvis Presley as the city's preeminent symbol. Each year in mid-August, around the anniversary of Elvis's death on August 16, the city celebrates Elvis Week, which brings visitors to Memphis from all over the world to pay tribute to the life and career of Elvis Presley.

With Graceland's stunning success, other Memphis historic treasures began rising, phoenix-like, from the ashes of the city's decline—Beale Street has been reborn as a vibrant musical destination, the original Sun Studio is now both a museum and a working recording facility, the Stax Museum is a replica of the old recording studio, the Peabody Hotel is once again the grande dame of the mid-South, and even the Presleys' Lauderdale Courts apartment has been restored. In some respects, the Memphis of today more closely resembles the one Elvis first experienced as a teenager than did the Memphis where he spent his final days. Today, even though some of the sites are lost forever, and efforts to restore some blighted parts of the city are slow, visitors who wish to see Memphis through Elvis's eyes have a plethora of places to experience.

The impact of Elvis on the city is also evident in the tributes that have sprung up—some even before his death. In January 1971, the stretch of Highway 51 South that runs past Graceland was renamed Elvis Presley Boulevard. Elvis Presley Plaza on Beale Street, across from the Orpheum Theatre, features a 10-foot bronze statue by artist Eric Parks, unveiled in 1980, representing the Elvis that so many remember: young, handsome, energetically strumming a guitar, that trademark sneer on his face, posed as if he's shaking his hips to the screams of an enraptured audience. Another famous Elvis statue is at the Welcome Center on Mud Island, a peninsula located within the city limits, bordered by the Wolf River harbor on the east and the Mississippi River on the west. Elvis statues have been erected in other sites across the United States and around the world—in Tupelo, Mississippi; at the Las Vegas Hilton; at the Municipal Auditorium in Shreveport, Louisiana; and even at his old barracks in Bad Nauheim, Germany.

Then there is the merchandise, which varies greatly in style and quality. Graceland is the mecca of officially licensed Elvis merchandise of all types, but you can find eclectic souvenirs and other tributes to the King at many places throughout Memphis, such as the Center for Southern Folklore, 119 South Main Street, near Beale; and A. Schwab's Dry Goods Store, the oldest continuously operating business on Beale Street.

One legacy that few other performers have inspired is an army of professional impersonators. Protest singer Phil Ochs may have been the first "official" Elvis impersonator, donning a gold lamé suit and singing Elvis hits for a crowd in 1970. There are now thousands of impersonators throughout the world, some amateur and some professional; some base their portrayals on the young 1950s Elvis, others on the flashier, heavier 1970s version. This is more of a Las Vegas phenomenon than a Memphis one, however. Memphis, appropriately, celebrates Elvis more as a local hero, an American success story that played out in its backyard, rather than as an overindulgent caricature.

Elvis's legacy also lives on in the charitable works for which he was known throughout his life. Whatever inner demons Elvis Presley battled, he was graced with a big heart and an unapologetically generous nature. Sometimes it manifested itself in big, flashy public ways, like his 1957 show in his hometown of Tupelo, Mississippi, to fund the Tupelo Youth Center; the 1961 benefit concert in Honolulu, Hawaii, to raise funds for a memorial for the USS *Arizona*; and a show in Jackson, Mississippi, in 1975 that raised $100,000 for victims of a hurricane. Stories abound of Elvis giving away new cars, expensive jewelry, and staggering sums of cash, not only to friends and employees but often to virtual strangers.

Memphis received much of his largesse. In 1964, Elvis purchased a yacht owned by Franklin Roosevelt and gave it to Danny Thomas to auction off, with the funds going to St. Jude's Children's Hospital. Elvis even contributed to the Memphis Zoo in Overton Park, donating a live wallaby that he had received as a gift from fans in Australia. Graceland has an entire exhibit devoted to Elvis's history of charitable giving.

As Elvis's death recedes in the rearview mirror of our collective memory, we have only the diminishing ranks of those who knew him to keep the firsthand stories alive. Colonel Parker died in 1997, Sam Phillips in 2003. Bernard Lansky still owns the Lansky Brothers clothing stores, and his son Hal, who rode horses with the Presleys at Graceland as a child, runs the day-to-day operations; Lisa Marie Presley, still a Lansky's customer and family friend, has carved out her own place in pop culture, both as a musician and as a tabloid fixture, the latter springing from her marriages to Michael Jackson and Nicolas Cage. Priscilla Presley went on to a successful acting career and marriage. Dr. Nick still lives in Memphis, albeit stripped of his license to practice medicine in the wake of the controversy over the cause of Elvis's death. At one point, he went on tour as a road manager for Jerry Lee Lewis and organized a touring exhibit of his Elvis memorabilia, including his medical bag. Various members of the Memphis Mafia and several of Elvis's old girlfriends pop up in the media every so often, telling tales of their time with the King and offering their perspectives on why he was the way he was and why his remarkable life ended as it did.

Although undeniably past its glory days as an incubator of new musical styles, Memphis continues to nurture a vibrant musical scene, especially for artists specializing in blues, R&B, country, and old-style rock, a list of genres whose diversity speaks to Memphis's hard-won multiracial identity. Although it may never produce another Elvis Presley, the city has ensured that neither he nor the music that inspired him will be forgotten.

Other large cities have famous natives, and others have strong musical traditions. But no other city is as associated with one legendary musical figure, and no other famous musician has had such a transformative effect on the city where he lived, as Memphis and Elvis Presley. If it can be said that Memphis made Elvis—that the King of Rock 'n' Roll was the product of the rich musical traditions that preceded him there—then an argument can also be made that Elvis and his legacy remade Memphis, providing the impetus for the city's ongoing revitalization. In his death, the King of Rock 'n' Roll gave the city a new life. Memphis gave Elvis Presley to the world; in return, Elvis Presley brought the world to Memphis. The hometown boy wouldn't have had it any other way.

Elvis Presley's presence is still felt throughout Memphis. This statue is the central attraction of Elvis Presley Plaza, a small park that overlooks Beale Street.

notes

chapter 1

3:    "What did I miss about Memphis? . . .": David Burlison, "Elvis, Justin Timberlake and Memphis," *Memphis Travel Examiner*, June 22, 2011.

5:    "The wooded bluffs . . .": <http://www.cityofmemphis.org/framework .aspx?page=296>.

7:    "War was not . . .": William Patton, *A Guide to Historic Downtown Memphis* (Charleston, SC: History Press, 2010), 14.

8:    "These dark days . . .": Ron McDonald, *Walking in Memphis* (Atglen, PA: Schiffer, 2010), 44–45.

9:    "Memphis's black citizens . . .": *The Tennessee Encyclopedia of History and Culture: Edward Hull "Boss" Crump*, <http://www.tennesseeencyclo pedia.net>.

12:   "Beale Street became . . .": *Historic Downtown Memphis*, 64–65.

13:   "Many people today . . .": *Historic Downtown Memphis*, 183.

15:   "The modern business . . .": Jamie Katz, "The Soul of Memphis, *Smithsonian*, May 2010.

chapter 2

18:   "Vernon had been . . .": Peter Guralnick, *Last Train to Memphis: The Rise of Elvis Presley* (Boston: Little, Brown & Co., 1994), 14.

20:   "Lauderdale Courts provided . . .": David Hoekstra, "Elvis Slept Here," *Chicago Sun-Times,* March 5, 2005.

28:   "In 1982, the city leased . . .": Ron Sitton, "Southern Culture: Beale Street Culture Blues," *The Southerner*, 1, no. 4 (1999), <http://www .southerner.net/v1n4_99/soculture4.html>.

29:   "What remains . . .": Interview with William Patton, September 30, 2010.

30: "Lansky's catered to the neighborhood . . .": S. S. Fair, "Clothier to the King," *New York Times*, September 23, 2001.

30: "Elvis Presley started coming in . . .": *Lansky Brothers: Clothier to the King* (Nashville: Beckon Books, 2010), 39–40.

31: "Elvis also came to Lansky . . .": John Christopher Fine, "The King and I," *Forbes FYI*, October 2005.

31: "In addition to being . . .": *Last Train*, 53.

32: "The original Peabody . . .": *The Peabody: A History of the South's Grand Hotel* (Memphis: Peabody Management, Inc., 2007).

33: "In 1965, it was sold . . . ": Author interview with Jason Sensat, Peabody Hotel Duckmaster, September 2010.

35: "This odd but much-beloved tradition . . .": *The Peabody*.

chapter 3

37: "Things began to happen fast . . .": *Last Train*, 52.

38: "Elvis continued to visit . . .": Bob Mehr, "Record Loss: More than a Music Store, Poplar Tunes Was Historic Landmark," *Memphis Commercial Appeal*, September 13, 2009.

39: "Visitors to the city . . .": "Poplar Tunes Sign Headed for Museum," *Memphis Business Journal*, April 6, 2010.

41: "Sun Records founder . . .": *Last Train*, 58–59.

42: "Marion and Elvis's conversation . . .": *Last Train*, 63.

46: "*Red Hot and Blue* was a mainstay . . .": Andy Meek, "Hotel Chisca Faces Possible Demolition," *Memphis Daily News*, June 9, 2006.

47: "Elvis was afraid . . .": Peter Harry Brown and Pat H. Broeske, *Down at the End of Lonely Street: The Life and Death of Elvis Presley* (New York: Dutton, 1997), 35–36.

48: "After WHBQ . . .": Ken Armstrong, "Chisca Hotel Faces Uncertain Future," *The Keystone*, June 7, 2006.

49: The "Overton Park Shell . . .": *Historic Downtown Memphis*, 179–82.

50: "In September 1954 . . .": Jim Hanas, "Strip Commercial," *Memphis Flyer*, August 5–11, 1999.

52: "Back in the 1950s . . .": Edwin Howard, "In a Spin," *Memphis Press-Scimitar*, July 28, 1954.

52: "The Eagle's Nest . . ." : <http://www.scottymoore.net/eaglesnest.html>.

53:    "Elvis, Scotty, and Bill . . .": *Last Train*, 118–19.

54:    "The original recording . . .": Sun Studio tour, September 29, 2010.

chapter 4

55:    "The *Hayride* was the main competitor . . .": Alanna Nash, with Billy Smith, Marty Lacker, and Lamar Fike, *Elvis Aaron Presley: Revelations from the Memphis Mafia* (New York: Harper Collins, 1995), 39.

56:    "Although Elvis's life . . .": Alanna Nash, *The Colonel: The Extraordinary Story of Colonel Tom Parker and Elvis Presley* (New York: Simon and Schuster, 2003), 75–90.

63:    "Perhaps the biggest treat . . .": Author interview with Jayne White, Sun Studio publicity director, September 29, 2010.

63:    "The first Elvis Presley single . . .": Ace Collins, *Untold Gold: The Stories Behind Elvis's #1 Hits* (Chicago: Chicago Review Press, 2005), 10–18.

64:    "The song was a risk . . .": *Last Train*, 235–36.

64:    "Elvis planned to settle . . .": Mark Medley, "Baby, Let's Play House: Inside 1034 Audubon Drive," *Dish Magazine*, August 5, 2011.

65:    "Considering Colonel Parker's original plan . . .": *Last Train*, 397.

65:    "To many today . . .": *Last Train*, 285–89.

69:    "Shortly after wrapping . . .": *Lonely Street*, 143.

71:    "In the 1950s, Houck's was unique. . .": <http://www.scottymoore.net/okhouck.html>.

chapter 5

75:    "In early 1957, Elvis's fame . . .": *Elvis Aaron Presley*, 96.

76:    "Golden recalled competing . . .": Dewey Webb, "The King and I: If Graceland Is Rotten to Décor, Don't Blame It on Elvis' Former Decorator George Golden," *Phoenix New Times*, July 28, 1993.

77:    "Elvis's primary concern . . .": Webb, "The King and I."

77:    "Even in a grand Southern mansion . . .": *Elvis Aaron Presley*, 96.

83:    "The chilly, drizzly weather . . .": *Lonely Street*, 150.

84:    "Down at Fort Hood . . . ": *Last Train*, 464.

85:    "At the end of the funeral . . .": *Last Train*, 475.

chapter 6

88: "The Colonel made the arrangements . . .": Peter Guralnick, *Careless Love: The Unmaking of Elvis Presley* (Boston: Little, Brown & Co., 1999), 96.

89: "The Claridge fell victim . . .": John Wood, "Memphis History Meets Modern Convenience in Claridge House," *Memphis Commercial Appeal*, May 31, 2009.

90: "Priscilla Ann Wagner was born . . .": Priscilla Presley with Sandra Harmon, *Elvis and Me* (New York: Putnam, 1985), 19–26.

93: "Another development . . .": *Elvis Aaron Presley*, 30.

94: "They were the *Memphis* Mafia . . .": *Historic Downtown Memphis*, 175.

95: "Although the Arcade . . .": *Elvis Aaron Presley*, 106.

96: "The Rollerdrome was part . . .": Vance Lauderdale, "Lost Memphis: Rainbow Lake and the Rainbow Rollerdrome," *Memphis Flyer*, September 12, 2008.

98: "In the late summer of 1962 . . .": *Lonely Street*, 253–54.

99: "Hard as it may be . . .": Robert Gordon, *The Elvis Treasures* (New York: Villard, 2002), 20.

100: "Ann-Margret's presence . . .": *Careless Love*, 152.

101: "Elvis met the boys from Liverpool . . .": Chuck Crisafulli, "Harmonic Convergence: When the Beatles Met Elvis—The Back Story," *Los Angeles Times*, June 7, 2009.

101: "Contrary to still-persistent rumors . . .": <http://www.elvis.com.au /presley/elvis_meets_the_beatles.shtml>.

103: "Over the years . . .": *Elvis Aaron Presley*, 228.

103: "Nichopolous was born in Pittsburgh . . .": *Careless Love*, 254; "Elvis's problem was that he didn't see the wrong. . .": Adam Higginbotham, "Doctor Feelgood," *The Guardian*, August 11, 2002.

106: "The only hitch . . .": *Lonely Street*, 333.

107: "Elvis saw the song . . .": Karen Meisenheimer, "Elvis a Civil Rights Pioneer? So Says UF Professor and Rock Music Expert," *University of Florida News*, August 4, 1997.

108: "As 1968 drew to a close . . .": Chris Davis, "The Swinging Sixties," *Memphis Flyer*, April 15, 2004.

109: "The Lorraine Motel . . .": *Downtown Memphis*, 170–73.

chapter 7

114: "In January 1969, Elvis recorded . . .": Editorial, "Elvis Faithful Can't Visit Site of His Last No. 1," *USA Today*, August 16, 2009.

115: "Elvis's opening night was a major . . .": *Careless Love*, 347.

116: "Elvis had developed . . .": *Lonely Street*, 347.

117: "About a month later . . .": <http://www.memphisheritage.org/mhi host/Accomplishment.html>.

120: "Elvis had a more lasting relationship . . .": *Careless Love*, 471–74.

120: "In between the stadium . . .": Piers Bigley, Larry Geller interview on Elvis Information Network, October 30, 2003, <http://www.elvisinfonet .com/geller.html>.

122: "The Memphis Mafia continued . . .": *Careless Love*, 173–77.

123: "Elvis trusted Geller . . .": Geller interview, Elvis Information Network.

123: "Two Memphis jewelers . . .": *Elvis Aaron Presley*, 481.

126: "Elvis's romance with . . .": *Elvis Aaron Presley*, 692.

127: "A turning point . . .": *Careless Love*, 608.

127: "When Elvis heard about the book . . .": *Lonely Street*, 367–68.

130: "The cause of death . . .": *Careless Love*, 652.

130: "The sordid details . . .": *Lonely Street*, 424.

epilogue

134: "Priscilla, Lisa Marie's legal guardian . . .": *Lonely Street*, 434; "he sold to RCA the rights to all the royalties . . .": *Careless Love*, 491–96.

136: "Then there is the merchandise . . .": *Historic Downtown Memphis*, 25.

137: "As Elvis's death recedes . . .": Author interview with Hal Lansky, September 30, 2010; "At one point he . . . organized a touring exhibit": "Doctor Feelgood," *The Guardian*, August 11, 2002.

credits

Cover: © Photofest

Maps: Designed by Kim Rusch

Page 2: Courtesy Memphis Chess Club

Page 16: © Photofest

Page 36: Beale Street, Humes High School, and Orpheum
© Mark P. Bernardo

Page 36: Sun Studio by dbking from Washington, D.C.,
(CC-BY-2.0) via Wikimedia Commons

Page 73: © Photofest

Page 74: Parker and Presley © Photofest

Page 74: Elvis in front of Graceland © Showtime

Page 86: © Photofest

Page 111: Both photos © Mark P. Bernardo

Page 112: © Photofest

Page 132: © Photofest

Page 139: © Mark P. Bernardo

Page 146: Courtesy Holly Reandeau

about the author

Mark P. Bernardo is the author of *Mad Men's Manhattan: The Insider's Guide*, also published by Roaring Forties Press. He is a professional magazine journalist and editor who has written about travel, entertainment, and luxury lifestyle subjects for such publications as *Stratos, Robb Report, Robb Report Motorcycling, Trump World, Stuff, Overtime,* and *Bloomberg Markets.* He was the editor of *Smoke* for six years and is the managing editor of *WatchTime*. A longtime Elvis Presley fan, he lives in New York's Hudson River Valley.

about the
MusicPlace series

Offering a new perspective on some of the greatest names in popular music, the MusicPlace series unravels the relationships between musicians and the cities they called home. Packed with details about the musician's life and work and stories about the city's neighborhoods and nightspots, each volume in the series captures the mood, the culture, and the sounds of a revolutionary era in popular music.

Other titles in the MusicPlace series include *Grunge Seattle*, *Jimi Hendrix: London*, and *Bob Dylan: New York*. Visit http://www.roaringfortiespress.com for details about our current and forthcoming titles, as well as to learn about author events, read reviews, and join our mailing list. Visitors to the website may also send comments and questions to Roaring Forties Press authors.

* * *